# THE ATTACK QUEERS

# THE ATTACK QUEERS

## Liberal Society
and the
Gay Right

RICHARD GOLDSTEIN

**VERSO**

London • New York

First published by Verso 2002
© Richard Goldstein
All rights reserved

The moral rights of the author have been asserted

1 3 5 7 9 10 8 6 4 2

**Verso**
UK: 6 Meard Street, London W1F 0EG
USA: 180 Varick Street, New York, NY 10014–4606
www.versobooks.com

Verso is the imprint of New Left Books

ISBN 1–85984–678–5

**British Library Cataloguing in Publication Data**
A catalogue record for this book is available from the British Library

**Library of Congress Cataloging-in-Publication Data**
A catalog record for this book is available from the Library of Congress

Typeset in Garamond by M Rules
Printed and bound in the United States
by R. R. Donnelley & Son

For Tony, my hearth

# CONTENTS

This book is written for two kinds of reader: straight people who know little about the queer community, and gay people who know even less about the progressive tradition. I hope other people will read this book as well, especially heterosexuals willing to acknowledge their anxieties about homosexuality. The full exploration of such feelings is a crucial step in gay liberation. But my main aim is to reach those who aren't aware of the rich connections between radical thought and queer sensibility.

In fact, the gay community is one of the left's great success stories, but little attention has been paid to that, or to the impact of queer thinking on progressive history. It's no surprise, in an era when anything unmarketable is ignored, that this connection should be absent from the repertoire of gay visibility. Nor is it surprising that populist myths of the people's march often omit the gay and lesbian contingent. But it seems all the more important to reclaim this connection now that it is threatened by the rise of a very different tendency.

Over the past decade, as right-wing rump movements arose in every minority community, a group of gay writers emerged to join the growing ranks of conservatives. These homocons, as I call them, claim to represent a "new gay mainstream," and armed with that contention they've ensconced themselves in the liberal media. I hope to show that this alliance between the gay right and liberal society is part of a broader backlash against the liberation movements of the past thirty years. For that reason alone, all progressives must take it very seriously.

In order to begin that reckoning, I want to answer a question that may never have occurred to many of my readers: Just what are the gay left and right? The answer isn't as simple as it seems. The usual criteria for calling someone liberal or conservative don't entirely apply in this community. After all, Camille Paglia is a registered Democrat; yet, for reasons I hope to explain in this book, I would place her on the gay right. For that matter, I once knew a bosom buddy of William F. Buckley who was as gayly progressive as he was staunchly conservative in the rest of his politics. From the moment the late Marvin Liebman came out to Buckley (whose response, according to Liebman, was to mutter: "Life is a vale of tears!"), this knight of the right reveled in the fact that he was now part of a new community in which the governing principle of sexual shame was suspended, and the traditional hierarchies of gender and sexuality gave way to a range of passionate and playful possibilities.

Liebman loved the ragtag results of this queer enterprise. Despite his staunchly right-wing beliefs, he saw no need to present himself as virtually normal. If anything, he was in flight from a world where masculinity and compulsory heterosexuality had confined him. Once he came out, he embraced gay life with such joy that I wondered whether his conservatism was merely a projection of his years in the closet. Would he have been a "San Francisco Democrat" if he'd grown up today? Perhaps, Liebman conceded, but the question was academic for a man in his sixties. Besides, he saw no contradiction between his free-market ideology and his pleasure in the nightly spectacle that unfolded around Dupont Circle, the queer nexus of Washington D.C. This ability to love your own in all their gonzo glory has been lost to Liebman's descendants on the gay right, whose sensibility is best described by a twist on the humanist slogan: Nothing alien is human to me.

The gay right represents more than a set of political convictions. It stands for an attitude toward queer culture and community. Indeed, it would replace the community as we know it with a more individuating model in which the mark of liberation is—to use the famous homocon phrase—"a place at the table." I want to show the heartlessness of this enterprise and the threat it poses not just to the gay political agenda but to the ethos that links us with feminism, multiculturalism, and the entire progressive tradition. I want radicals outside and inside the gay movement to understand the implications of the homocons' rise. This is not just another tribe in the ever-expanding queer nation; it's a highly articulate attempt to secede from that confederation. Aided and abetted by a powerful cultural backlash, the gay right is on the march. Unless it is met by a compelling response from the other side, its impact will alter not just the lives of queer people but the future of the left.

As a journalist, I'm trained in the craft of rapid reaction. For more than thirty years, I've tried to make sense of the uncanny or outrageous on a deadline. My beat is located at the intersection of sex, culture, and politics. Wherever that nexus leads, I follow. At *The Village Voice*, America's oldest and largest alternative weekly, I've covered the counterculture of the 1960s, the sex wars of the 1970s, the AIDS crisis of the 1980s, the impeachment scandals of the 1990s. But the most enduring trend I've chronicled is the steady flight of the middle class from the radical project of liberation. I've always believed that, if the gay movement succeeded, its members would be tempted in the same direction.

But this retrenchment is by no means inevitable. Fluidity is the essence of middle-class life. The same impulse to recoil from change also draws these people to its ecstatic energy. My ambition as a journalist is to keep that attraction alive by contesting the backlash before it becomes entrenched. That's my goal in taking on the gay right, and because I believe such responses are most effective when they're prompt, I've written this book on a very tight deadline.

That wouldn't have been possible without Gretchen Dukowitz, an adept and intrepid researcher. I thank her and the

Gay and Lesbian Alliance Against Discrimination, which helped me find her. Bill Dobbs was a generous source of information, as was the policy institute of the National Gay and Lesbian Task Force. I thank that group for inviting me to its Creating Change conference, where I saw that an alternative to the gay right's vision is not only possible but alive and well. I'm grateful to my comrades at Verso: Niels Hooper, who held production to give me extra writing time; Amy Scholder, whose discerning editing greatly expanded the scope of this book; and Colin Robinson, who believed in it at the start. *The Village Voice* was a proving ground for many of these ideas, and I thank them for letting me fly. I'm grateful to Lawrence Bloom, Howard Cruse, and Ed Sederbaum for their enduring support, and to Mark Boal, my fellow word warrior, who urged me relentlessly to make the leap from journalism to the far more complex task of writing a book like this. (Plus, he passed the truest test of friendship by loaning me his laptop when mine crashed.)

I'm indebted to many queer writers for my approach to this subject. But I've been inspired particularly by the rigorous compassion of Eve Kosofsky Sedgwick and Michael Warner, and by the democratic ethic of gay historians such as Allan Bérubé, George Chauncey, John D'Emilio, Martin Duberman, and Jonathan Ned Katz. The writer with the greatest impact on my sensibility (though she bears no responsibility for my ideas) is my friend and former colleague Ellen Willis. I owe much more than this book to my partner, Tony Ward. Not only did he put up with months of bleary logorrhea, but he helped me to distill the babble. As indispensable as his emotional presence has been, his grounding in activism and anthropology is the model for my intellectual life.

Finally, a word about wording. There are more ways to describe us than are dreamt of in your philosophy. In addition to the generally acceptable terms *lesbian and gay*, there are the bisexuals, the transgendered, the intersexed, the questioning (a label that probably describes any reasonably sensitive adolescent), and other words that specify ethnically derived identities, such as *two-spirit*, an American Indian term. The attempt to be inclusive explains why the acronym that identifies our community sounds like an Albanian surname. As an alternative to LGBT, LGBTQ, or LGBTQI, there's the recently rehabilitated *queer*. Unlike *gay*, this word denotes alienation from the norm, so it might even apply to heterosexuals who feel that way. (Sedgwick has used it to describe herself, though she's married to a man.) *Queer* also has ideological connotations, mostly involving links to other oppressed groups; whereas *gay* carries a more distinctly tribal edge. It's deeply ironic that this word has been appropriated by the virtually normal, since it was originally applied to prostitutes (as in "gay Paris"). But labels are like drag; their "realness" is relative.

I'm drawn to *queer* as a logo—if not as garlic to wave in the gay right's face—but that might mean changing familiar phrases such as *gay liberation* and *gay rights*. So I've decided to use these terms in a somewhat arbitrary way. By *queer*, I mean the whole gestalt, including sluts, punks, s/m dykes, trannies, sissies, sailors on leave, and Anne Heche. By *gay*, I generally mean out and proud homosexuals. But don't hold me to these definitions. At the risk of offending or confusing some, I've done what feels right. Why else would I be . . . a major 'mo?

1

## THE LIBERAL EMBRACE

Queers have two masters, neither in leather. Both of them boast that they are fair, as most masters do, but only one claims to be a friend. This is the liberal, who welcomes our company and supports our fight for civil rights. The other master is willing to grant us the basic entitlements of citizenship, at most. This is the conservative, who promises to respect us, or even to love us, but only in the absence of our sin. The difference between these two masters is hardly insignificant, given the clash between them known as the culture wars. Queers play a central role in that ongoing conflict, and our lives reflect the dual reality it has created in America.

For us, it is the best of times, it is the worst of times. A mere thirty-three years after cancanning queens held off the riot squad at Stonewall, queers are a staple of entertainment and a rich market niche. Nearly half of the American people live in cities or states with gay rights laws. More than a quarter of America's largest corporations offer domestic partner benefits. Pride marches that were once processions of defiant visibility are now carnivals drawing millions around the world. A recent *New Yorker* cartoon sums up the response in urban society to this surfeit: "You're here, you're queer," says a weary sophisticate. "We're used to it." Yet, beneath the blasé attitude, a deep ambivalence persists.

Our legal status is more ambiguous than that of any other American minority. The Supreme Court has yet to recognize a constitutional right to be gay, and so our civil rights are revocable to an alarming degree. Sodomy is still a crime in thirteen states, where this designation can be used to bar us from certain professions or deny us access to our children, on the grounds that we are members of a "criminal class". Nor are sodomy laws merely symbolic. In Texas, the President's home, two men (an interracial couple, naturally) were arrested last year for having sex in private—and convicted of the charge. Yet they could have watched that same activity on cable TV. Such is life in the charivari of uncertainty.

As we frolic through the nation's living-rooms, more than a hundred antigay bills are pending in state legislatures, and major efforts to repeal gay rights ordinances are underway in Houston and Miami. Federal law, which applies to even the most enlightened enclaves of America, creates a maze of contradictions that can trap even the most adept of us. At this writing, same-sex partners of 9/11 victims still don't know whether they qualify for federal survivor benefits, because the regulations are deliberately ambiguous in that regard. Thousands of gays and lesbians go through a less dramatic version of this ordeal when they leave jobs that provide domestic partner benefits. Their partners aren't eligible for the low insurance rates offered by COBRA because the Defense of Marriage Act, which applies to this federal program, bars same-sex couples from taking advantage of it. What a contrast with Western Europe, where the culture wars have been fought and won by the left. Within the European Union, domestic partnerships are widely recognized, gays and lesbians serve in the military, and homosexuality is nowhere a crime. These social democracies have become the guarantors of our freedom, but in the land of the free we are subject to the rules of the road, which vary enormously.

Oppression may not weigh heavily on boys who brunch, but it haunts the queer poor, who must navigate a social service system that refuses to recognize their existence. Homophobia may not be a clear and present danger in elite universities, but it's a recurring nightmare in the average American high school. And even in gay-friendly circles, those who don't fit the gender mold suffer under a system best described by a variation of the old motto about race: If you're gay, it's okay; if you're queer, disappear. Yet even the most secure of us will likely be the victim of bigotry at some point. When a lover's bequest is withheld, when child custody is denied, when a hospital leaves decisions about a dying partner to her distant relatives, when a friend's practice fails because the clients think he looks too gay, when a longtime companion is left off the guest list at a family wedding, when the cocktail hour is punctuated by a homo joke: At such moments we are rudely reminded that under the finesse, we're still faggots. Despite claims to the contrary, all of us inhabit a halfway house that calls itself freedom.

Like so many stigmatized groups before us, we gravitate to large cities where the friendly master rules. But even our liberal allies are fearful of our presence in their midst. The difference that defines us seems contagious, especially to those who have invested a great deal of energy in managing their desires, and the very fact that the sexual line can be crossed marks our acceptance with a special anxiety. Yet the liberal's self-image requires that such fear and loathing be denied. The result is a roil of conflicting emotions culminating in a welcome. This is the liberal embrace, and it produces a similarly anxious response in its recipients, one that veers between rebellion and a clinging to convention, cock-eyed optimism and a lingering feeling of living on parole. These are the poles of queer consciousness in liberal society.

The straight corollary to this mixed mood is a fascination with all things queer that coexists with homophobia. The same hip public that revels in genderfuck also lauds Eminem, convinced by critics that there's something heroic about his harangues, something playful in the standing ovation he gets for shouting: "Hate fags? The answer's yes!" Here, the feelings liberals have taught themselves to deny are fully exercised. Whatever guilt might attend that release is defused by the queer who attests to its harmlessness. When Elton John appeared at the Grammy Awards last year to perform a duet with Eminem, he gave a fey imprimatur to a pop culture that bashes as it blesses, and expects its targets to cooperate.

The literary version of this vaudeville is provided by gay writers who assail their own kind. Call them attack queers. They owe their success to the liberal press. Andrew Sullivan is the major gay voice at *The New York Times*; Camille Paglia is the queer queen of *Salon.com*—now joined by the latest lesbian sensation, Norah Vincent, who also appears in the *Los Angeles Times*. Though these pundits have more than gay issues on their mind, all of them made their mark in the 1990s by assailing the "orthodoxies" of queer life. It was an exciting spectacle for liberals tired of radical queers telling them what was wrong with straight society. How sweet it was to see the radicals attacked—and by their own queer kind. These heterodox homos of the right played the same role as rapine rappers, providing a sadistic *frisson* hard to come by in polite society. No wonder attack queers have flourished in the liberal press. They're as bad as liberals wanna be.

A similar backlash has occurred in black and feminist writing, but progressives in both communities are still widely heard from. That's not the case when it comes to us. A left-leaning lesbian like Deb Price of *The Detroit News* reaches far fewer readers than any homocon. Queer radicals can publish in *The Nation* and *The Village Voice*, but these weeklies have a much smaller circulation than a paper of record like the *Times*. And since the *Times* and similar mainstream publications are the most visible venue for gay writing, their fondness for attack queers means that gay opinion in America is skewed to the right. Progressives play a prominent role in queer culture and politics, but not in the mass media. Here, writers who oppose key items on the gay rights agenda, such as anti-bias legislation, have the loudest voices. It's as if the liberal press had designated a black foe of affirmative action like Ward Connerly as the spokesman for his race.

Yet political ideology isn't the main reason why homocons are such a hot commodity. Their claim to fame is dissing gay types that threaten straights, such as sissies, sluts, tribal dykes, and the ultimate sexual outlaws, trannies. Under the banner of "common sense," they mock anyone who lives outside the orbit of respectability. If there's a motive for this assault, it has less to do with gay rights than with assimilation. Job number one for homocons is promoting the entrance of gay people into liberal society. But this deal comes with a price. It requires gays to maintain the illusion that we're just like straights, and precisely because this image is a pretense, it must be upheld by shaming those who won't play the part. Attack queers target these unassimilable homos, thereby affirming the integrity of heterosexual norms. They perform a valuable service for liberal society by policing the sexual order. If they weren't so viciously efficient at this task, they would never have gotten where they are.

*A Place at the Table* is a seminal work of the gay right. Its author, Bruce Bawer, argues that most homosexuals desire just that, and that they're no different from the other guests (except, perhaps, for a subtle twinkle in the eyes). Yet despite the appeal of this idea to straights, the mainstream media have all but passed Bawer by.

Because he's critical rather than contemptuous, he isn't ready for prime time. Other homocons have suffered a similar fate. For example, Jonathan Capehart is a black conservative whose editorials for *The New York Daily News* helped win that tabloid a Pulitzer Prize, but he hasn't benefited from the attack-queer boom. Neither of these writers has the claw-hammer touch of Sullivan or Paglia. Neither is eager to engage in the cat fight that passes for hot gay prose. Neither has speculated, as Paglia has, that Matthew Shepard asked for the fate that befell him by cruising straight men. Neither has mocked gays who flame, as Sullivan has. This gift for the homophobic *aperçu*—made acceptable because it comes from a homo—is the key to success for queer writers in the liberal press.

Consider Norah Vincent's meteoric career. Her first major piece appeared in 1996 during Sullivan's tenure as editor of *The New Republic*. It was the umpteenth screed against lesbian groupthink, complete with the hoary rejoinder "Get a sense of humor," but its unabashed contempt struck a nerve. Soon Vincent was part of the stable at *The New York Press*, a hip right-wing alternative weekly. There, her inaugural feature was an attack on gay male sexuality set at a circuit party, as these all-night dances are called. Adopting the classic tabloid pose of the "normal" observer, Vincent slipped through the crowd, recoiling from the pumped bodies and orgiastic ambiance. Her brutal tone perfectly suited the backlash tenor of the *Press,* which ran Vincent's piece on page one, prompting a boycott from gay groups.

For Vincent, this protest was propitious. Soon, she was

recruited by the *Press*'s more powerful competitor, *The Village Voice.* Its editor was looking for a writer who would challenge the paper's progressive image, which Vincent quickly did. Her first feature, a profile of a transsexual, focused ghoulishly on the surgical aspects of gender reassignment. Again she was rewarded with a cover, this one featuring an illustration of a Barbie's body being sheared. Activists picketed the *Voice*, but it only added to Vincent's notoriety. She became the subject of a profile in *The New York Times*, and then she was snapped up by *Salon*. These days, she can be seen on *Politically Incorrect* sparring with the waggish host Bill Maher. No lesbian or gay writer has had a more rapid rise.

Sullivan was more than a mentor to Vincent, he also served as a model for her attack-queer stance. Though he brags that he never bashes individuals, Sullivan specializes in clobbering unregenerate queer types. Take his account of a recent visit to San Francisco's Castro district. Here, Sullivan encountered streets "dotted with the usual hairy-backed homos. I saw one hirsute fellow dressed from head to toe in flamingo motifs." Readers of his website can attest to Sullivan's revulsion at gay styles that depart from the norms of male presentation. He's appalled by camping, prancing, or any expression of effeminacy. Back in the bad old days, this contempt for the femme was the mark of an upwardly mobile homo, just as lesbians who aspired to acceptance fled from the butch. Stonewall challenged all that, but now gender conformity has returned as a marker of upward mobility. For Sullivan, drag is more than just unmanly; it's déclassé.

If there's one thing Sullivan hates more than flaming, it's "the libidinal pathology" of queer life. He's hectored gay men for their obsession with "manic muscle factories," and railed about their dedication to "a life of meaningless promiscuity followed by eternal damnation." It took a scandal revealing that he advertises for unsafe sex on the Internet (under the screen name RawMuscleGlutes) to get Sullivan to change his tune. Now he argues that gay men should reclaim promiscuity as part of their masculinity. You'd never know that he broke into *belles lettres* by advocating same-sex marriage as the only alternative to a life of "hedonism, loneliness, and deceit." But consistency is the hobgoblin of small glutes.

Sullivan's contradictions are masked by a fluent style and a gift for provocation. It was a shock to open *The New York Times Magazine* in 1996 and discover his cover story claiming that the AIDS epidemic is almost over in the gay community. It was astonishing to hear him proclaim in *The New Republic* that HIV-positive men can bareback without risking reinfection. Or to hear him argue, in a lecture sponsored by the *Times,* that gays would do better to carry guns than rely on hate-crime laws. (He even cited Martin Luther King as a supporter of armed self-defense.) As these examples illustrate, Sullivan is not a systematic thinker. Nor is he particularly original. If he has a gay following, it's largely among those who know little about their community's history—and how can they be blamed, given the silence of straight society?

Since the founders of the modern gay movement aren't part of the pantheon of American civil rights leaders, not many people are aware of Harry Hay and Del Martin. Nor do most high schools teach their students about Harvey Milk, the first openly gay elected official, who was assassinated in 1978 by a conservative colleague on the San Francisco Board of Supervisors. So how can young people be expected to understand why Sullivan's reading of gay liberation is akin to a skinhead's take on Zionism? The problem is compounded by the media blackout of those who could correct the record. The relative obscurity of queer leftists means that Sullivan is likely to be the first gay writer a young person encounters after coming out. Most readers of his breakthrough book, *Virtually Normal,* are unaware of Michael Warner's very effective radical rejoinder, *The Trouble With Normal.* And Sullivan refuses to debate his critics. Better to rail at the left from the safety of his website than to subject his ideas to scrutiny.

Without a working knowledge of gay and lesbian history, it's impossible to see through the simplifications in *Virtually Normal.* But the ideas Sullivan ascribes to some elite academy of the post-modern left go back long before queer theory. Ever since homosexuals were identified as a deviant type in the nineteenth century, we've identified with other sexual outcasts. The first words we used to describe our milieu were borrowed from the argot of prostitutes. We were "in the Life" before we were in the phone book. Michel Foucault did not invent the idea that as long as there's a norm there will be queers, drawn to each other by a common experience of difference. This concept was central to the code that came with our identity. But as grounded as we are in this sense of distinction, we've also been drawn to the belief that gay people are just like straights "except for what we do in bed," as the old homophile saying goes. This duality creates an abiding conflict between those who demand the freedom to be otherly and those who pursue the right to be normal. In the gay movement, these factions are called liberationists and assimilationists. The ideological ramifications of their clash have shaped queer politics for much of its history.

The first modern gay organization, the Mattachine Society, devoured itself in a struggle between radicals and conservatives within a few years of its founding in 1948. As McCarthyism advanced, the rads were purged, at great cost to the group's growth, but they regrouped to lead a second wave of agitation after the Stonewall rebellion of 1969. No sooner did this new movement get off the ground than it split again over whether queers should join the revolution or stick to a gay agenda. The former actually seemed possible when the Black Panthers embraced the Gay Liberation Front (an event you won't see in a Spike Lee film). But the momentum favored the more parochial Gay Activist Alliance. Its focus on queer issues, its tactics (such as "zapping" the enemy with squads of kissing guerrillas), and its Saturday night dances held in an abandoned Manhattan firehouse—the first gay disco—were much more pleasurable than building socialism, which, as Oscar Wilde once quipped, takes too many evenings.

When AIDS began its long march, the sexual component of queer politics became much more pronounced. Now the battle lines were drawn around the zipless fucking to be found at bath-houses and cruising grounds. Radicals rushed to defend these venerable gay institutions, while other activists joined the effort to shut them down. But this sex war was part of a larger struggle between assimilationists and liberationists—or, in the parlance of that time, suits and sluts. The issue of normalcy hovered over the safe-sex debate that raged throughout the 1980s, and it still informs the radical queer critique (as in Warner's analysis of sexual shame and its relationship to social hierarchy). Indeed, the current clash between the gay right and left is a politicized update of the conflict between suits and sluts.

It's a war that may never end. Yet the movement has been remarkably successful at incorporating rads and trads, probably because most of us belong to both camps at once. We feel normal *and* different. Queer culture deals with this double vision by keeping one eye on liberation and the other on assimilation. The ethos it embraces is not virtual normalcy but a new way entirely. Call it radical diversity.

The gay right has a fine time listing the cadres that assemble, each under its own banner, at a typical gathering of the tribes. Whatever your worst nightmare, you'll see it on flagrant display. Yet one value ties this unruly amalgam together: the determination to be the person you always wanted to be. This is the dream of drag kings and homothugs, lipstick lesbians and leather men, radical faeries and even gay Republicans. The queer community aspires to be a safe space for all these types, as well as each new cadre that comes along, complete with a righteous attitude and a new vocabulary. This roster of identities attests to the centrality of self-determination in the ongoing project of liberation.

Even queer theory, in its thorniest deviations from conventionality, embraces this ideal. Eve Kosofsky Sedgwick, a major voice on the queer left, speaks of "allosexuality," the arrangement of many variations of desire without a hierarchy. In other words, we are most free to be ourselves when we are least organized around the socially determined poles of straight and gay. You may believe that this thinking defies reality, but you must concede that it's a brief for freedom. The group-think libel has its uses for the gay right, but in fact radical queer sensibility creates strong-willed individuals with (all too) high self-esteem.

Identity politics can make any queer conference a Balkan adventure. Acronyms expand exponentially as new groups assert themselves. (Can you say "children of partners of people of trans-identified experience"?) But these terms describe real people, and the movement allows them to represent themselves. This nurturing of diversity stands in stark contrast to the model offered by the homocons. Theirs is a single, morally correct way to be gay. No caucus of vegan leather men could approach this uniformity. The look may not seem regimented—normalcy never does—but imagine a march called by the gay right. The sea of white faces would be a less louche version of the crowd on Fire Island during its pre-AIDS heyday. The affect would be manly all around, with the few women in attendance channeling the spirit of Ayn Rand in their demeanor. And the ethos would be a wholesome version of the classic gay clone code: No freaks, femmes, or feminists who aren't funny need apply.

Rigidity is a common reaction to anxiety, as the gay right demonstrates. They deeply fear difference, including their own. No wonder they don't feel queer.

There have always been homosexuals on the right. But until recently most of them thought like Joe McCarthy's gay henchman Roy Cohn, who died of AIDS insisting he was heterosexual. The climate gay liberation created has made it safer for conservatives to come out, so their numbers in the community have grown. But they never constituted the gay mainstream, and they still don't.

It's hard to pin down the ideology of gay people—much more is known about our consumer tastes—but voter exit polls provide a clue. Regardless of class and gender, gay voters are as loyal as Jews to the Democratic Party, and far more likely than straights to call themselves liberal. They lean left on bellwether issues such as immigrant rights and gun control, notwithstanding the rod fixation of the gay right. They even support school bonds. What's more, the gender gap that is such a feature of American political life doesn't apply to gay men. They tend to vote like straight women. (Despite the image of lesbians as progressive, the voting record shows them to be slightly more conservative than gay men.) The homo version of the angry white male exists primarily among attack queers.

Still, gay voters have been known to switch sides when it suits them. In the last presidential race, about a million voted for George W. Bush. Of course, Al Gore did three times as well, but the lesson wasn't lost on the Republicans. For some time now, key figures in the party of Pat Robertson have been urging a suspension of hostilities toward homos. Even Ralph Reed, who put the Christian Coalition on the political map, now advises his Republican clients not to "concentrate disproportionately" on lashing the legions of Sodom. And by that standard, Dubya is a friend of Dorothy.

Bush has made several gay appointments, and quietly left in place Bill Clinton's executive order banning antigay discrimination in the federal workplace. But he's also pushing a faith-based initiative that would fund religious groups despite their refusal to hire gay people. Thousands of homosexual clients could face bias from these church-run agencies. And it remains to be seen whether Bush will address the homophobic aspects of his welfare package, especially when it comes to penalizing single parents— that is, *all* gay parents in the eyes of the law. He has yet to endorse any new piece of gay rights legislation, and as long as The House of Representatives remains in Republican hands, he'll be able use the strategy he followed as governor of Texas, when he avoided vetoing such bills by preventing them from ever reaching his desk.

Bush took just this tack to kill a hate-crimes bill that included sexual orientation. He's called gay rights "special rights" and sodomy statutes "a symbolic gesture of traditional values." He would shake the hands of homocons, but not object to their arrest for having consensual sex in the State of Texas. And he's willing to play the queer card when it suits his purposes. Last year, the Bush administration tried to cut a secret funding deal with the antigay Salvation Army, until *The Washington Post* blew the whistle. During the presidential campaign, Bush firmed up his shaky right flank by backing a move to deny the Log Cabin Republicans, an association of gay conservative political clubs, a booth at his state party's convention. Yet homocons regard him as a suitor. There's a country music lyric that describes such misplaced affections: Looking for love in all the wrong places.

Just as Log Cabinites are enchanted by winks and smiles from the right, the queer community is charmed by the idea of gay Republicans. It's the ultimate proof of the old gay lib saying, "We are everywhere." And there's a general willingness to give homocons the benefit of the doubt, if only because they speak out against hardcore phobes in their party. Reflecting this consensus, the Gill Foundation, a major (and largely liberal) gay funder, has given seed money to several gay right groups. But this largesse hinges on an image that homocons take pains to maintain by presenting themselves as something other than conservative. Their favorite buzzword is *independent.*

This is a cover right-wingers often assume when romancing liberal constituencies. So it's no surprise to find a clearing house for anti-feminists called the Independent Women's Forum, or its homo equivalent, the Independent Gay Forum. Its purpose, as its website proclaims, is to "lay out the intellectual groundwork for an opening to the center." But its online archive holds all the evidence necessary to prove that these homocons are anything but centrist. Here are briefs for the ultimate oppressed class: "pale white males"; attacks on a sissified community that "clutches oppression like a security blanket"; manifestos for a new movement that would allow gay men to "focus on gay male issues." Were it not for the pesky issue of sexuality, these views would not trouble a conservative shock jock. Think of Rush Limbaugh with monster pecs, and you've got Andrew Sullivan.

Compared with Sullivan's he-man harangues, gay Republican rhetoric reeks of gentility—or it did until recently. Earlier this year, a new think tank spawned by the Log Cabinites placed an advertisement in major papers accusing the movement's leadership of demanding "employment anti-discrimination laws and hate crime protections" while flocking to "RSVP cruises, packing warehouse circuit parties, and filling black-tie dinner halls to hear keynote addresses from Hollywood celebrities." If you can get past the puritanical sniping, here is the homocons' central argument against gay rights: We don't need anti-bias laws since we don't really face job discrimination. "The truth is, most gay people are not victims, at least not in the economic sense," Sullivan writes. "Instead of continually whining that we need job protection, we should be touting our economic achievements . . . and politically focusing on the areas where we clearly are discriminated against." The real problem, he insists, is "the denial by our government of basic rights, such as marriage, immigration and military service. In this sense, employment discrimination is a red herring."

Not to the 97 percent of lesbians and gay men who feel subject to it, according to a recent Kaiser Family Foundation survey. The gay right insists this perception doesn't reflect reality; they call it "virtual victimization." But there's nothing virtual about the discrimination experienced by more than half of gay people in the Kaiser sample. Twenty-three percent report major problems in housing and employment. Even Bruce Bawer writes about being fired from a right-wing publication when his sexuality became known. In that respect, he has something in common with the real gay mainstream. In poll after poll, passing anti-discrimination laws is a top priority.

Homocons point out that queer complaints are only a small fraction of the cases handled under local anti-bias statutes. There are many reasons for that, including fear and shame, but it doesn't mean these laws are useless. They provide crucial protection for people in "sensitive" professions such as teaching or youth counseling. They will be crucial if the faith-based initiative becomes law. And they create a momentum against discrimination, making it less likely that the next generation will suffer from homophobia to the same degree. But it may always be true that the onus grows greater the poorer or queerer you get. By fighting for anti-bias laws, the movement represents all its members, not just pale gay males.

Heretics and homosexuals are always seen as wealthy—it rationalizes the resentment. But queers have a harder time than even Jews convincing people that poverty exists among them. The cliché of fey affluence certainly fits the image many gay people are eager to project. (After all, in America, living well is not just the best revenge; it's the only one.) But this profile is based mostly on data collected by market researchers. By correcting their bias toward people who live in upscale gay enclaves, read slick gay publications, drive Subarus, and shop at Ikea, sociologist Mary Virginia Lee Badgett has discovered an undetected planet queer.

It turns out that the average gay man earns *less* than his straight male counterparts. Lesbians do no worse than straight women (who typically earn less than men), but two women living together are likely to have a much lower income than the average heterosexual couple. This is not to mention the economic straits of queers of color, transpeople, and other sexual outcasts. Poverty is the only dirty secret left in our community, and it lends itself to the negligent reasoning that is Sullivan's specialty.

Still, upwardly mobile gays (or guppies) are here, if not queer, and they have their own issues. They may not feel vulnerable to discrimination, but even the most accepted among them can't have a spouse. Homocons have honed in on this inequity, and used to it stake their claim on the center. Sullivan doesn't help his case when he dismisses job bias or disses identity politics, but when he contends that marriage is an inalienable right, most gays are with him, if only because they know it's a right they are denied.

In addition to its power as an organizing tool, the marriage issue has allowed the gay right to marginalize the left by misrepresenting its ambivalence as opposition. Certainly there are plenty of radicals who think *no one* should marry—or, in any event, that the state should have no say about intimate relationships. Feminism and gay liberation have produced a compelling critique of matrimony, but it would be hard to find a progressive who thinks only heterosexuals should be allowed to apply for marriage licences. The most profound difference between rads and trads on this issue involves the freedom to make other choices. As Foucault writes: "We have to understand that with our desires, through our desires, go new forms of relationship, new forms of love, new forms of creation." For the queer left, liberation creates an opening to explore these possibilities. There are as many relational options as there are affinities, and as long as these unions are consensual, they should be honored one and all.

What is queer normalcy? Read Bruce Bawer to find one answer; listen to Rufus Wainwright to encounter quite another. One lives a life of partnered contentment; the other plunges into affairs that leave him musing, "Everything I like is just a little bit dangerous." Think of Anne Heche and her identity migrations, RuPaul and his gender modulations—or, for that matter, Mr. RawMuscleGlutes, also known as the author of *Virtually Normal.* There is no queer way. The variations in our relationships are as complex as our identity. Homocons are out to replace this fabu flexibility with a single model. And they won't stop at rehabilitating the individual. Their ultimate ambition is to abolish the queer community. In the new Jerusalem they are building, there is no such thing. "You have no secret rings or rites, no distinct set of values," writes gay conservative Dale Carpenter. "You're only an individual who must make your own way in the world, unable to depend on the safety of belonging to an elect tribe."

It seems impossible to image gay life without community. But for much of our history, that's been the case. In fact, the queer community is a relatively recent creation, and it would never have taken the shape it has without the vision of gay leftists.

Homosexuals have never really depended on the kindness of strangers. Ever since we were cast as outcasts, we've been forming networks that were more than merely sex or friendship circles. In the 1950s, when police felt free to break up "rings" of perverts, there was a panic in liberal circles over something called "the homintern" that allegedly controlled the arts in New York. Several years before Stonewall, *The New York Times* noted with a mixture of curiosity and dismay that deviants were becoming more visible. It wasn't just the flaunting that unsettled them, but the early signs of a new social formation. These creatures of the shadows were beginning to think of themselves as a bona fide minority.

Still, no one could have predicted that 100,000 "avowed homosexuals" would descend on Washington in 1979, or that three times as many would return eight years later. By the millennium, these marches had morphed into festivals complete with partying, protesting, praying, and shopping on a grand scale. Mainstreaming has corrupted the movement, many leftists rage. But the fact remains that these events are the largest gatherings of gay people in the history of the world. They aren't just political rallies but celebrations of the very idea that we are a community.

The nexus of this nation is a vast web of affinity groups representing virtually every religion, profession, avocation, and obsession. There are thousands of these groups and hundreds of local institutions—community centers, newspapers, social and sexual venues—as well as several dozen national organizations pursuing aspects of the same basic agenda. The whole heap coheres without a central hierarchy. It's like a lava light, popping up in endlessly morphing shapes. You don't have attend the Michigan Womyn's Music Festival, join Al-Fatiha (the gay Muslim group), call yourself an s/m activist, or run with Transsexual Menace to be part of this society. If you're queer, there's a place for you in the acronym, if not at the table.

This convergence didn't occur by chance. Nor was it merely the product of historic changes. The mass uprooting of Americans during World War Two brought thousands of formerly isolated homosexuals together, as gay historians Allan Bérubé and John D'Emilio have noted. But the community that emerged was a deliberate creation, based on the premise that people with a common experience of stigma are *a people*. This was not a widely held belief in postwar America. It was a Marxist idea, as was the concept that oppression can be overcome only through the creation of an alternative identity. But no one can do that alone. It takes a community to liberate a person, and so gay lefties set about building one.

Harry Hay was a member of the Communist Party USA in 1948, when he thought of organizing homosexuals. At the time, they had many names but no formal sense of themselves as a society. "They were the one group of disadvantaged people who didn't even know they were a group," Hay has written. He was the first to call queers an oppressed minority.

Hay began by forming a small organization on the Communist model, complete with semi-secret cells. He called it the Mattachine Society, deriving its name from the medieval sect of jesters and fools who played a crucial role in skewering orthodoxies, including the reigning concept of gender. A lesbian group, the Daughters of Bilitis (named for a mythical associate of Sappho), soon joined the fray. It started as a social alternative to lesbian bars, but it soon became political, and that's when the surveillance began. At early DOB events, reports historian Lillian Faderman, "everyone was aware that there was always the possibility of a police raid." No wonder the group remained small. "Most middle-class lesbians, to whom DOB tried to appeal, had no desire to expose themselves to such harassment."

As for Hay and his comrades, they headed for the gay beaches of L.A. where they tried to organize, only to be hooted away. Within a few years, Hay's nascent movement followed suit by expelling him. He retreated to the role he still occupies, as an utterly original source of insight into queer consciousness.

Decades before queer theory, Hay was hailing gender variance as a revolutionary force. To look at photos of him bedecked in Western jewelry, and perhaps a skirt, is to glimpse a truly self-made American, Marxism and all. Yet the great irony about Hay's gay politics is that it owes much more to democratic socialism than to communism. Marx took pains to distinguish his "scientific" ideology from the beliefs of radical utopians, whom he tellingly called "men of the rear." Marx knew that a number of them were homosexual.

If Hay is the father of gay liberation, just as Del Martin and Phyllis Lyon are its mothers, the closest thing we have to a grandparent is Edward Carpenter. This nineteenth-century British socialist believed that "homogenic love" could subvert the class system, and usher in an era when cooperation trumps competition. If that sounds like a tract from some gay socialist cadre, it should. The revolutionary potential of same-sex love was a tenet of utopian socialism, especially for Oscar Wilde. What could be closer to a gay manifesto than his statement that, just as Know Thyself was the exhortation of the ancient world, "Over the portal of the new world, 'Be Thyself' shall be written." There was no room for product placements in this program. Wilde believed that "true individualism" could be achieved only when property had lost its hold on personality, and that could happen only in a liberated society.

The queer community is often regarded, by its friends and foes alike, as a quintessentially American invention—and so it is, right down to the labrys pendants and Mr. Leather pageants. But this creature has a European lineage. It may owe its soul to the sexual revolution of the 1960s, but it was born some forty years earlier, during the Weimar Republic's heady days. The German Socialists were the first party to organize homosexuals, and to that end they sponsored a bill decriminalizing sodomy. Its ripple effect produced the most vibrant queer society the modern world had ever known. Based in Berlin, it was some 350,000 strong, and it supported more than two dozen publications as well as theaters, a bowling league, and even a stamp-collecting club. Berlin's queer nightlife is what survives in the popular mind—after all, you can't make a musical from a Philatelic Society—but there was also a gay political movement complete with warring factions, and an explosion of sexual identities.

Weimar's queer community was different from ours in several key respects. For one thing, lesbians were much more visible and varied in their styles; for another, sexual separatism was not the order of the day. But in many ways, Weimar was our womb: the first place where informal networks of gay people coalesced into a true community. It could only have happened in a culture that regarded this process as a healthy expression of freedom. No wonder it was one of Hitler's first targets. Shortly after the Nazis took power, they sacked the institute founded by the queer movement's best-known leader, Magnus Hirschfeld. Though he escaped, his movement was crushed—but only temporarily. The idea that sexuality can be the basis of a community survived and thrived in liberal societies. We are the waking incarnation of this socialist dream.

*

It's not just a reflex that prompts many gay people to vote liberal even when it doesn't reflect their immediate interests. It's the ghostly imprint of these remarkable gay radicals. The model they created is imbedded in our community; indeed, it *is* our community. To enter it is to be located on the left. If gay people are ever to be weaned from progressive values, they must lose their sense of community. And so, homocons set out to make us feel ashamed of this "security blanket." To participate in pride parades and other ritual observances of identity is a sign of weakness rather than a source of inspiration. On a playing field growing ever more level, there's no need for membership in a special society. In fact, it may actually stand in the way of our rise. After all, there's only so much room at the table. Liberal society is not prepared to make a place for the whole *mishpuchah.*

"Once we have won the right to marry," Sullivan has quipped, "I think we should have a party and close down the gay movement for good." What would queer life be like if this vision ever comes to pass? The movement would be smaller and more splintered, assuming it survives. A wealthy gay elite would pursue its own interests, petitioning the government for what Sullivan calls "civic equality," but not demanding legal redress for discrimination. Of course, not everyone would feel so sanguine about bias, but the neediest among us would have the least access to funds and publicity. A marginalized progressive faction would be all that represents queers who need civil rights protections most. We would know the meaning of Billie Holiday's observation "God bless the child that's got his own."

But the most dramatic changes would flow from the individuation of our social life. Without its communal ethos, gay culture would revert to what it was before Stonewall. Bitchiness would be an art form again, as the attack-queer style became a chic expression of contempt for anyone outside the virtually normal fold. The traditional hierarchies of gay society would return with a vengeance. The inappropriate—formerly known as "obvious"—would occupy a lower social rung, as would those who qualify as sluts. There would be even less contact between the races, outside of sex. Gay bonding would no doubt remain, but its instrument would be what it was before we were a community: networks of friends. Sullivan has written movingly about the power of gay friendship. It's not a new idea. Friendship is the great solace in a host of queer classics, from *The Boys in the Band* to *Dancer from the Dance.* In plays and novels about AIDS, friendship is vitally important, but hardly sufficient. As these works make clear, in times of crisis, community equals survival. But this concept has a special use for queers, even in calmer days.

Few of us get a true sense of what it means to be gay from our families. We aren't raised with the skills to navigate the Life. Before there was an LGBT entity, each generation had to make its own queer way. Though we developed very effective codes, if only to recognize each other in a hostile world, nothing transmits social information like a community. The way we greet each other (by kissing instead of shaking hands), the way we hold our bodies today (so different from the stressed-out stylization of pre-lib days), the special tone in our voices (not feminine or masculine, but gay), the distinctive way we combine protest and partying, the rainbow flag we wave: All this has less to do with homosexuality than with community—and all of it can be lost. There's nothing eternal about this creation of ours. Like everything constructed, it can change beyond recognition, or even collapse.

Not that the queer community is fragile. It has withstood countless conflicts over gender, identity, and sexual practice. Why have these schisms never succeeded in tearing us apart? The answer may have less to do with our loyalty to one another than with our relationship to straight society. Ever since Stonewall, our demand for recognition—not just as individuals, but as a group— has been a *casus belli* of the culture wars. But both sides in this conflict share an uneasiness about homosexuality, especially when it reaches a critical mass. Camping is one thing; community is quite another. A lesbian commitment ceremony is touching, a lesbian legion terrifying. This ambivalence means that, under the right circumstances, even liberals might like to see the rainbow flag replaced by the Stars and Stripes.

The schisms of yore never appealed to this impulse. Why would straight liberals want dykes or trannies to form *more* communities? You couldn't keep up with all the pride parades. Even the recent notion of post-gay never caught on with straights, since the last thing they need is the collapse of boundaries that distinguish them from us. It's different with the gay right. They speak directly to the contradictory climate of our time. Theirs is a conservative philosophy that appeals to liberals. It may reject the concept that gays are a people, but it advocates their integration into civic society. This is a deal liberals have always offered the other. It summons up the Enlightenment and it doesn't frighten the horses. As agents of this accommodation, homocons carry the imprimatur of liberal society. That is their special strength—Liberals are no less fearful than conservatives when it comes to homosexuality, but they see us in a different light. The right regards gay people as emblems of a sinful culture that is undermining the nation and the family. Liberals don't feel unduly threatened in that respect; indeed, they are willing to welcome us into full citizenship, as they have other pariah groups. For them, the issue isn't our sexuality but our sensibility and the distinctiveness it generates. Liberals fear for their place in the world true pluralism would create. And so, the bargain they set requires us to deny our difference, thereby affirming the bedrock principle of liberalism: that all people are fundamentally the same.

Many minorities have colluded in this illusion, at great cost to the cultures that sustained them in their exile from respectability. But ever since the 1960s, the issue of suppressing difference in the name of assimilation has been front and center for radical politics. It lies at the heart of every liberation movement, including ours. On what terms shall we meet the majority? For queers, this question haunts our emergence—and it accounts for the tension that lingers in the liberal embrace.

2

## THE HOMOSEXUAL GENTLEMAN

In 1984, James Baldwin gave me one of his only interviews about homosexuality. The most important black writer of his generation had maintained a virtual silence on this subject that clashed with the candor of his prose. After all, Baldwin was one of the first Americans to write a major novel with a gay relationship at its core. He could still recall his publisher's first reaction, in 1955, to *Giovanni's Room*: "I was told I was a young Negro writer with a certain audience, and I wasn't supposed to alienate that audience. If I published the book, it would wreck my career. They wouldn't publish the book, they said, as a favor to me."

It was an old story in 1955: a talented gay artist enjoined from offending liberal folks by forcing them to deal with homosexuality. But Baldwin wouldn't take invisibility lying down. Instead, he took his book to England, where it appeared to rave reviews. Only then was it deemed fit to print in America. At first glance, this reluctance seems odd, since the taboo on gay fiction had been broken by Gore Vidal eight years earlier. But Vidal was white. It was one thing for him to sanction sodomy, quite another for a black man to insinuate that racism and homophobia were intimately linked; that both expressed a fear of the body and of love.

In imagining an alternative to this reign of terror, artists like Baldwin invented a new reality. Yet the old rules still governed him when it came to talking about homosexuality. Black gay artists of the Harlem Renaissance had shown a similar reticence. They were obliged to represent their people's most "human" traits, and in the 1920s that rubric certainly didn't include perversion. As late as 1963, white racists used this issue to demean the March on Washington by revealing that one of its organizers, Bayard Rustin, had been arrested for solicitation. But Martin Luther King Jr. stood by his lieutenant, making a connection between racial and sexual justice that would inspire a generation of black leaders to form alliances with gays. By 1984, the time for Baldwin to break his silence was long overdue.

Perhaps he was aware of the stomach cancer that would kill him three years later when he agreed to meet with this writer from *The Village Voice*. Sitting at a Greenwich Village joint that had been a boho hangout in his time, but was now a sports bar, Baldwin seemed dismayed. He hadn't counted on being surrounded by brew-belching jocks who didn't know him from Adidas. Still, he wasn't here for the fauna. He had all sorts of questions about the new world that sprang up during the years he'd spent living mostly in France. What was a gay clone? Why did these men wear hankies of different colors in the back pockets of their jeans? What was AIDS, and how did it spread?

I ventured to explain the clone look, deciphered the erotic hanky code, and gave him a quick course in safe sex. Baldwin's lack of savvy surprised me, but I could see that he was alive to the tragic contours of the epidemic and the gripping contradictions it presented—the specter of mass death alongside the image of liberation. And so I had many questions for him, the most pressing of which involved the intersection of homosexuality and race. White gay men like me flamed with rage at the straight world, but I noticed that my black gay friends handled their feelings differently. They, too, were angry, but not at the black community; and the way they behaved "uptown" was not quite closeted, but not exactly out. What accounts for this difference in attitude and demeanor, I asked Baldwin? Why am I so much more pissed-off than they?

A small smile crossed his face as he replied: "Well, I think that's because you are penalized, as it were, unjustly; you're placed outside a certain safety to which you think you were born. A black gay person is already menaced and marked because he or she is black. The sexual question comes after the question of color. It's simply one more aspect of the danger in which all black people live. I think white gay people feel cheated because they were born into a society where they were supposed to be safe. The anomaly of their sexuality puts them in danger unexpectedly. Their reaction seems to me in direct proportion to the sense of feeling cheated of the advantages that accrue to white people in a white society."

I've never heard a more insightful explanation for the enduring enigmas of gay life. It won't displace the gay gene theory, but Baldwin's concept of entitlement does account for the fact that people of different races and classes tend to express their homosexuality in distinct ways. It explains why black gay men might choose to be "on the down low" rather than out and proud like their white peers, or why blue-collar dykes traditionally favored flaming butch and femme personae over the more muted middle-class lesbian model of gender respectability. It even speaks to the differences between the homo sexes. Lesbians are said to be more progressive, more faithful, and more group-oriented than gay men because—well, women are like that. But what if these famous traits have less to do with biology than with a certain relationship to danger?

People who don't feel safe in the world—and who find security only in their communities—are likely to reflect (or refract) communal values down to the way they think of sexuality. But when community is the *source* of a danger that isn't supposed to exist, the reaction is a vehement rejection of orthodoxy. The pain of stigma, for those who aren't raised to expect it, is a stunning source of radical energy. No wonder the gay movement first arose among the fierce females and fallen males of the white middle class. No wonder their response to lost entitlement was to rage against the hetero machine.

Of course, the cadres of gay liberation never imagined that

straight society would be so quick to embrace them. They didn't reckon that the street around the bar where they fought Alice Blue Gown would be renamed Stonewall Place, that their crime against nature would become a source of entertainment, or that the stereotypes they skewered would be so promptly replaced by "positive" images. The fussy flit would morph into a sitcom sidekick, guy Friday to the female lead; the killer queen would be rehabilitated as the homo down the hall, a bright-eyed embodiment of decency with a small dog. Still, visibility would have its limits. On no account could a gay man be shown flying a fighter jet or wielding an M-16. A dyke might get the girl, but only until the right man came along. Queers could be victims or valiants, but never aggressors—except when it came to bashing their own.

Baldwin knew the dark side of social mobility all too well. He had fled from the gay world precisely because of its ceaseless backbiting and its terror of being cast with the oppressed. All that would change with liberation, I assured him, but I could tell from his pained expression that Baldwin sensed otherwise. He knew that race was the fulcrum of stigma in America, the onus that couldn't be managed or marketed away. Next to that, the "problem" of homosexuality was negotiable. It had arisen in the middle class and it could be resolved there, the way so many other issues were. Give queers their own cable network and they'll call it freedom. Perhaps that was why Baldwin chafed at my enthusiasm for the gay movement. He saw its promise, but he sensed that, when all was said and done, many middle-class gays would leap at the chance to reclaim their entitlement. As a permanent resident in the land of stigma, he had seen countless groups begin that same precipitous rise: *per aspera ad* assimilation.

Eight years after *Giovanni's Room*, a very different but no less subversive book, called *Stigma*, appeared. In this slim volume, the sociologist Erving Goffman demonstrated that the specifics of a difference—be it race, religion, disability, or sexual deviance—were less significant than the common patterns of behavior all these traits produced. To read Goffman is to see the relationship between gays and other groups that possess "an undesired differentness from what we had anticipated." There's only one fundamental distinction among all these "soiled identities": Some are based on visible qualities, while others involve "blemishes of character" that may not show. As a result, there are two kinds of stigmatized people: the discredited and the discreditable. Homosexuals fit into both categories, since some look the part while others don't. Closeting our difference makes us merely discreditable. My queer cohort—the Stonewall generation—was the first to come out because we *chose* to, and when we did, we suddenly entered the world of the discredited.

We never set out to behave like straights. We were interested in messing with the codes of sexuality; in beard glitter, amazon flannel, jism and genderfuck. Nothing irked us like the desperate pretense that homosexuals were an elite. What could be more pitiful than an aristocracy of the air? We had earthier things to worry about, such as writing under our real names, landing permits for our parades (then the largest illegal gatherings in America), getting the phone company to list our organizations under the unmentionable word *gay*, fending off the men who would froth at the sight of us holding hands, and—job number one—getting the cops off our backs.

That was relatively easy. By the late 1970s, sodomy had been decriminalized in the states where most of us lived, and homosexuality disappeared from the manual of mental illnesses. You could no longer hang a sign that read "fairy swatter" over a hatchet, as the owner of an Irish bar in Manhattan learned when it was invaded by ululating queens. As long as we remained within the gay belt of major cities, we were free to create our own culture, and this we did with a flagrant flair that was the envy of straights. The result was that cult of the stigmatized known as disco, with its gay inflected divas, its anthems of survival, and its imagery of sexual plenty. Of course, there was no comparable interest in lesbian culture, with its complex ties to feminism and its raging debate over separatism. Women's bars existed, but they hardly proliferated, and rural lesbian colonies were not the hot center of the new gay visibility. Still, it was a great time to be queer—at least on the surface. But there was a reason why our enclaves were called ghettos. A hidden melancholy confirmed the perception that we hadn't liberated ourselves from oppression, only created a glittering world apart.

At work, at family events, or whenever we interacted with straight people in anything less than a critical mass, the old code asserted itself. There was a price for being out and proud. It meant living with endless tension, enduring the tight smiles of friends and colleagues suddenly faced with a problem they never expected to encounter, and managing these interactions with painful artifice. Even worse was the toll we had to pay for simply existing, since, as Goffman notes, "tolerance is usually part of a bargain." Being gay meant learning the art of subordination known in those days as feminine grace. The reason gay men had such close female friends wasn't because they understood women, but because they recognized the role women were expected to play.

Yet despite these rich alliances, gay men who could pass but chose not to were never consoled for losing their entitlement. There's something ironic in forfeiting the "privileges" of femininity—which may be why there are so many great lesbian comics—but for most gay men, losing male power was no joke at all. Straight men compelled homosexuals to make a choice between faggotry (servitude) or fighting back, and the latter carried the risk that comes when any subaltern male acts uppity. The gay equivalent of lynching meant being murdered in some grotesque and implicitly erotic way, like the unsung victims of "homosexual panic" who were stabbed, choked, bludgeoned, castrated—rarely just shot dead. This was what could happen to pushy fags, but the alternative seemed even riskier.

Each of us had grown up knowing someone who bought the bargain of subordination and bore its weight: the pansy who did hair, the bull dyke who drank the day away, the kid who couldn't throw a ball and failed to fight when called a sissy. These outcasts wore their status in every stylized gesture they made, giving them the brittle or hysterical look that was associated with their kind. There was nothing natural about these tortured styles; they weren't butch or femme but the effect of being sentenced to a quotidian version of Kafka's penal colony, where the name of your crime is slowly carved into your body by a machine.

From the closet, I looked upon these convicts with horror, knowing that the secret I kept about myself was all that stood between me and the penal colony. But I was already living under the sentence of repression. I might have grown old in its confines, passing its effects on to a family, if I hadn't come of age when an air of insurrection made it possible to imagine kicking out the jams. Still, I didn't come out until nearly ten years after Stonewall, when I fell in love with another man. It shouldn't have been earth-shaking in 1979, but it rocked my world.

All my straight male friends backed off (though not the women in my life), leaving me to make my way in a strange gay milieu. It look me several years to realize that the clones around me, whose singular look reminded me of industrial carpeting, were actually quite faceted, and often very loving. But the hardest task was one all gay men faced: dealing with the impact of our transgression. I'm talking here about the effect on heterosexual men who could no longer count on faggots to affirm the sexual code. Every institution that depended on male hierarchy felt the shock of queer refusal, and the reaction was typical of the way men respond to panic: hysterical rage of a sort I'd encountered only in my nightmares of what it might mean to be gay.

I can still remember when the danger I dreaded became real. In 1994, a small contingent of Irish gays insisted on marching in New York's St. Patrick's Day Parade, and for that one year they got away with it. I joined them as a reporter, and so did the city's first black mayor. The combination of black power and queer visibility sent this rowdy crowd into a frenzy. We strode past a million people shrieking epithets. It was a terrifying spectacle, but utterly exhilarating. By facing stigma in all its fury, I was finally able to see the system it created, and how crucial my suffering was to its cohesion. I was the sexual other against which masculinity could be defined, just as blacks were the key to whiteness. Without these outcast identities, the entire order might collapse. This was why subordination kept us safe, and coming out made us targets: As Baldwin would later tell me, we were called faggots "because other men need us."

At some point in the march, the mayor turned and said: "I feel like I'm in Mississippi." Yet he, too, seemed elated, and I understood why. We were seeing "the naked lunch at the end of the fork," as William Burroughs describes such moments of truth, and it had a galvanizing effect. For the first time, I felt the same inside and out—and there were new, unexpected allies to behold. As the crowd howled, I noticed girls in Catholic school uniforms giggling and waving at us. I'm sure Baldwin would have understood why this line from a blues song popped into my head: "The men don't know but the little girls understand."

If we had thought more about the structure of stigma, we might have understood how its terrible logic shaped our psyches, and even our desires. We might have blamed our parents less. And we might have deduced that stigma is a tar baby, which adheres no matter how you move. Hypernormal behavior, pleas for acceptance, heroic feats, and acts of defiance: All were noted by Goffman as typical responses of the outcast. Our most cherished gestures of liberation confirmed our status. Out of the closet, we were still stuck to the tar baby.

But that was the last thing we wanted to hear. We were the warrior generation, convinced that selfhood could be willed into being. Reality could be altered in a burst of revelation, like a popper high. It was terribly middle-class (hadn't Marx snickered: "For the bourgeoisie, ecstasy is the mood of the everyday"?), but for all our revolutionary ardor, we preferred to ignore such social facts. We were too busy building a world without classes, races, or even sexes. There was no room to reckon with the feelings of regret that attended our loss of birthright. What we needed was to come together, and in order to serve that tribal purpose we devised our own creation myth. This was the coming-out story. It had little to do with social reality, but it was very inspiring.

The painful stirring of an unwanted attraction, the eerie sense of not being from where you're from, the feelings of implacable isolation and impending doom: all were swept aside in the glorious moment of coming out. But missing from this story—as it always is in heroic sagas—was any sense of the ambiguous social situation our emergence had created. Though male violence continued to haunt us, most of us were now living in relative safety. Pockets of tolerance appeared in liberal society, and as these free zones expanded it was suddenly possible to imagine respectability. Yet this shift in decorum was hardly liberation. We were still defined by our difference. The word *queer* perfectly described our new status as resident aliens, and in the 1980s it was proudly adopted by the gay generation that came of age in the world we had wrought.

This wasn't a place where we were "free to be you and me," but neither was it the penal colony. It was a halfway house where the penalty for our crime was not inscribed on our bodies but insinuated in the way straight people met our gaze. The proliferation of "avowed homosexuals" made it even easier to identify us as the other, and so our visibility actually helped the system of stigma to cohere, as did the perception that it was now based on more humane terms. AIDS accelerated this process by marking our difference—often with an actual stigmata in the form of a skin lesion. Yet the epidemic also revealed us to be fully human and worthy of rehabilitation. Now we could apply for the parole other pariah groups had received, and some time during the age of Clinton (who bore his own mark of infamy), it was granted. We were given a chance to prove that even people with soiled sexual identities can play a useful part in society. Once we passed this test, we might attain true freedom. We were being offered the promise of a life where our difference made no difference.

The official mood of liberation hadn't prepared us for this

option. Our militance made it hard to see the depth of our need for reconciliation, and now that it actually seemed possible, many of us leapt at the chance. Of course, not all queers felt this temptation. Whole classes of us were visible but not by choice; they were "menaced and marked" from the start, as Baldwin would put it, and it gave them a jaundiced perspective on assimilation. But we who had propelled ourselves out of the closet were more like fallen aristocrats than a minority whose members had been raised to expect bias. It was the warrior generation's dirtiest secret, but most of us were middle-class before we were gay; we'd known the primal feeling of safety, and, oh, how we wanted it back! Could we return to the social womb? It depended on the bargain we struck with the only part of the straight world willing to admit us: liberal society.

A new gay type would emerge to meet this embrace: the homosexual gentleman. There were lesbian ladies, to be sure, but their rise was less notable than the sudden shift in status of these formerly downcast men. They had always existed, but they could never be out without risking their respectability, and their strained attempts to reconcile their lives with the Life were often subject to brittle mockery. Now, as these gents advanced from the shadows to the front lines of assimilation, they were no longer ridiculous. They were poignant, but only to those who could see the futility of their position. Their devotion to the powerful, their dedication to the normal, their zeal for in-group purification, their lust for upward mobility: all had the quality of a familiar part played before an ambivalent audience. In this social drama, as Goffman writes, "a phantom acceptance provides the basis for a phantom normalcy."

There's a joke that bears repeating here: "What's a kike? A Hebrew gentleman who's just left the room." The subject of this wisecrack is decorum and its discontents. It concerns the moment when the bearer of a soiled identity comes face to face with the normal. Goffman calls it "one of the primal scenes of sociology" because, in this breathless encounter, "the causes and effects of stigma must be directly confronted by both sides."

Both parties know that the difference between them isn't real in any essential sense, yet both are bound to observe the hierarchy it creates. The result is a ritual of honorific words and respectful gestures signifying something other than equality. This etiquette is the way to manage a difference so crucial that it cannot be ignored, yet so absurd that it cannot be addressed. The parvenu must resolve the paradox by meeting the terms of a hard bargain. He or she must behave in a way that minimizes the difference while making it apparent. The classic product of this painful arrangement is the Hebrew gentleman of the nineteenth century, who could be identified by his surname but not (if he could help it) by his manners. The homosexual gentleman—out and proud, but not obvious—is his direct descendant.

Every time I hear Andrew Sullivan say that gays are more like Jews than blacks, I flash on my parents' insistence that Jews are white. When they were growing up, that was a wish rather than a generally agreed upon fact. In truth, Jews are a mélange, but we could hope to be white in America because a different pariah group, blacks, had been selected as the racial other. In Europe, it was different; Jews were the racial other, and we paid the price. Homosexuals, on the other hand, are the *sexual* other. Our stigma has nothing to do with race, so it plays out differently. Gay men—and, for that matter, lesbians—are more like women than like any minority.

Yet there *is* a link between gays and Jews in the nature of our difference: It may or may not show. We can manage our deviance or flaunt it, and so we all, in some sense, volunteer for the role we play. What's more, our identity is a living dissent from traditional Christian probity. This explains why the enemies of gays are often the same folks who were once the foes of Jews. My parents grew up when anti-Semitism was a respectable bias, and when a priest named Father Coughlin could rail against Jews on the radio. It's deeply ironic that his descendant should be Dr. Laura, a devout Jewish woman who uses her faith to justify homophobia. But in America, the ambiguities of status make it inevitable that those who have recently achieved respectability will bash those who have only just arrived.

If American life is an endless struggle for prestige among groups that have felt oppressed at some point in their history, the appearance of a new people affects them all. So it's likely that the recent rise in Jewish status—especially among fundamentalists— was prompted by the emergence of gays. There's no need to see Jews as Satan's spawn when homosexuals can serve as the demonic force that defines virtue and makes the faith cohere. By the same token, the public scolding Jerry Falwell received when he blamed 9/11 on gays may reflect the sudden selection of yet another pariah group: Muslims. It would be a profound irony if we queers owed our newfound modicum of safety to the danger others must face, but that's the American way. The most common treatment for stigma is to pass it on to someone else.

Europeans are more constant in their calumny, as Jewish history attests. But the Enlightenment blazed a new trail for this emblematic pariah group, in some ways more torturous than any they had trodden. This was the rocky road of assimilation so tellingly described by Hannah Arendt in her classic study of anti-Semitism. To read Arendt's account of this ordeal, which ended in genocide, is to glimpse the dark side of the deal now being offered to gays. Not that we queers are subject to the same encrusted image of evil. But there's something about the bind Jews were forced to bear as they entered liberal society in the nineteenth century that should give homosexual ladies and gentlemen pause.

At the dawn of assimilation, Arendt writes, most Jews "lived in a twilight of favor and misfortune, and knew with certainty only that both success and failure were inextricably connected with the fact that they were Jews." As a gay man in an ostensibly tolerant age, I know this same reality. My career has been shaped by it, and so has my social life. Every encounter with a heterosexual involves expectations that arise from my sexuality. No matter what I write about, this fact will occur to the reader who is aware of it. If my identity becomes known to the straight man with whom I'm conversing, his words will carry a certain formality beneath which I can read anxiety. Every now and then, I get the eerie feeling that my life as a queer is set in the Jewish past.

I'm especially aware of this time warp when I leave New York, where both Jews and gays are visible enough to make me feel at home. I recall one such excursion, a guest appearance at a rural campus during which I was peppered with questions like "Does God love you?" (as an atheist, I was sure He must). That night, I visited the local gay bar, far from town. With its windowless exterior and barely lit sign, it had the look of a place that wasn't out to advertise. But inside, it was more like a refuge than a dive, and far more sexually mixed than the bars I'd known—a *shtetl* with a jukebox. Yet through the music, I could hear the periodic crash of bottles thrown from cars racing by. The crowd seemed oblivious to this racket—people started singing the disco hit "It's Raining Men!"—but for me it meant that the refuge was also a target. An almost primal determination kept me from leaving, but I flashed on the classic Jewish response to such situations, one my parents uttered as an ordinary expletive: "*Oy, gevalt!*" Oh, violence!

Of course, life is different in liberal society. People are punished for gay-bashing, and the f-word is banished to locker rooms and other Ur-zones of male bonding. But the halfway house is not just a place of safety; it's also where the pariah learns to be a parvenu. This lesson involves much more than manners. It means taking on a new personality whose major purpose is to assuage straight anxiety. At the heart of this kabuki is the ability to represent a norm you cannot realize. The parvenu Jew apes Christian mores; the gay arriviste embraces heterosexual values. This preserves the illusion that stigma can be overcome by good behavior. But there's a trick clause in the contract: As Goffman notes, the bearer of a soiled identity "should fulfill ordinary standards as fully as he can, stopping short only when his efforts might give the impression that he is trying to deny his difference." It's precisely this distinction that maintains the order.

Gay men have different social obligations than lesbians. After all, women don't construct the male order; men do that. So lesbians can fade into the female landscape—in fact, they're advised to, and the more evident they are (as in hardcore butch), the less likely to rise. But gay men are expected to be identifiable so that the order can cohere. Playing the faggot is the classic way to meet this demand, but assimilation offers another—presumably less degrading—option. Gay men should be out, but not outrageous. It's the mark of a homosexual gentleman to be open about your identity, but not to throw it in people's faces by flaming with kinky (kikey) traits.

"A man in the streets, a Jew at home," was the motto of the nineteenth-century Hebrew gentleman. There's a similar maxim that suits today's gay arriviste: "Butch in the streets, femme in the sheets." Both sayings boast of a benign solution to the problem of difference: keeping it private. But the apposition of man and Jew (or butch and femme) betrays the shame that comes with passing. A heightened fear of mortification shapes the parvenu mentality, and it's never more vivid than in the panic that ensues when someone "obvious" comes into sight. The reflex persists long after the most brutal effects of stigma have been overcome. I feel it when I see a Hasid on the subway, and I suspect the gay gent feels it when he spies a drag queen. That itchy *frisson* is the well-founded fear of being polluted by your own kind.

All the elements of parvenu style—its capacity for infighting, its obsession with presentation, its devotion to hierarchy, and its contempt for those who deviate—are present in Andrew Sullivan's writing. But this sensibility existed long before he was a gleam in the liberal media's eye. The attack queer dates from the pre-lib days, when dishing was an art form. Larry Kramer transformed this type into a literary persona. Kramer was no homocon; if anything, he was a kind of gay nationalist with a bounty of rage toward straights. But he reserved his greatest wrath for his fellow queers, especially of the promiscuous persuasion. The AIDS crisis made Kramer's jeremiads against promiscuity read like matters of life or death, and they were publicized as precisely that. Yet there was something suspect about the way the liberal media lauded any gay writer willing to be critical of queer mores as "courageous."

The attention wasn't lost on Michelangelo Signorile, the publicist turned gay activist who made a shtick of the attack-queer style, churning out breathlessly bitchy tirades with the point made in manic UPPER CASE!!!!! The attack mode was a flexible instrument that could be just as effective against closeted celebrities as it was against unrepentant sluts. In the 1990s, when gossip became the most important journalistic form, Signorile found a way to dress its cruelty in the mantle of activism. He wielded the ultimate weapon of the supermarket tabs, the homosexual exposé, and gave it a militant new name: outing. Arguing that public figures who cling to the closet are poor role models, Signorile attacked members of his kind who weren't obvious *enough*.

Outing became a guilty pleasure of the mainstream media. It was voyeurism rehabilitated as politics, and the attack-queer style was part of the fun. But this vaudeville would soon be subsumed in an even more compelling show: the pageant that allowed liberals to let their resentments show. Attack queers were the perfect enablers of this cultural backlash. In the name of truth-telling, they expressed all the nasty thoughts about homos that had only recently become unmentionable. Their ostensible mandate was to challenge the "orthodoxies" of identity politics, but their tone, which veered from withering to sadistic, expressed the real intentions of this entertainment. Reading their outbursts against flaming creatures and other unregenerate queers was like peering into the liberal id.

Of course, frank homophobia was still unacceptable, and so was self-hate. But few straights would object if attack queers created a sense of shame around the things that most distinguished gays from straights: not just sex, but community. There was a realpolitik of repression at work here, but it could be acceptable to liberals only if it were articulated by the oppressed themselves; then it was not bigotry, but tough love.

And so, as the century turned, a new persona emerged in the liberal media. In the gay-friendly *New York Times*, Andrew Sullivan raked gay liberation over the coals. In raffish venues like *Esquire*, Camille Paglia railed against radical lesbian thought (which she described as "a tendency toward the inert"). In the alternative press, sex columnist Dan Savage lit into the concept of tribal pride, identifying it as one of the seven deadly gay sins. The liberal media drew the line at queer skinheads in England and Canada who took to beating up gay activists: That went beyond minstrelsy—just barely.

All this bore a more than passing resemblance to the late-1990s ideology known as post-gay, which arose as a reaction to the cheeky alienation expressed by the term *queer*. Post-gay ladies and gents didn't feel queer; they didn't even feel particularly gay. They were individuals first, homosexuals only when the sap flowed. There was a radical potential in this stance, one that appealed to the idea of sexual mutability that animated queer theory. In the mind of a British critic like Mark Simpson, the concept of a gay identity actually inhibited the homo possibilities. (It certainly didn't describe the men who had sex with each other in an officially homophobic environment like the military.) But in the hands of James Collard, the British editor who had just been hired to run the American gay monthly *Out* (replacing a lesbian feminist), post-gay meant something very different than fighting the oppression of categories.

Collard is the kind of journalist whose prose runs purple at the sight of merch, and as the gay market beckoned, his moment

came. "Anger no longer has the power to unite us," Collard proclaimed at a 1998 panel sponsored by *Out* to introduce him to
the New York gay media world. "We no longer see our lives
solely in terms of struggle." As he inveighed against the movement and on behalf of people too busy making dinner for their
boyfriends to be bothered by activism, the audience balked. The
specter of AIDS was still too vivid to allow for such insouciant
revisionism, and Collard was nearly hooted off the stage. He
soon returned to England, and the post-gay movement
foundered. But it had signaled the emergence of a new gay class
whose values and interests clashed with the queer sensibility.

These gays had grown up with the sense of entitlement
Baldwin spoke of, but unlike my generation they never lost their
birthright by coming out. Their families accepted them, and so
did their bosses. There was still a risk in being gay, but for them
it was a distant fear that could easily be overcome by the smiles of
straight friends. Yet a nagging perception of vulnerability
remained. The best response to these feelings was to deny them.
Collard had been right to tell his New York audience that these
gentlefolk "no longer see their lives solely in terms of struggle."
They didn't dare to. And they were looking for a philosophy to
help maintain the mood. Post-gay was the first attempt to claim
them, and though it fizzled, it served as a trial run for the gay
right.

One reason why post-gay failed to catch fire was the cool
reception it received from the mainstream media. It was one
thing for respectable gays to reject the queer movement; quite

another for them to leave the category of gay behind. That was the last thing liberals wanted. It was hard enough to tell gays from straights; whole nuances of fashion and body language arose around this problem. (One popular belief held that you could tell a guy's sexuality by the way he danced: Hands below the waist meant straight; hands above meant . . . fuggedaboutit!) But sexual selection was only one reason why it was crucial for gays to be known as such. The distinction kept the sexual order intact, and it was up to the parvenu to maintain it by full disclosure. The same requirement had been presented to Hebrew gentlemen more than a century before. As Arendt wrote, these parvenus "had to differentiate themselves from 'the Jew in general' and just as clearly to indicate that they were Jews. At no time were they allowed simply to disappear among their neighbors."

Jewish exceptionalism (like its black equivalent, "the talented tenth") meant that only educated or gifted individuals could qualify for social acceptance. It's the same with gays who petition for a place at the table today. They must prove above all that their arrival doesn't signal an invitation to every common queer. After all, there are only so many slots for gay pundits, business partners, or party guests: too many homos and the whole place stinks of sodomy; too many dykes and there's no place for the Man. This fear of a queer planet isn't just a rationale for limiting competition. It also speaks to the primal nature of prejudice, and the secret knowledge that anyone's identity can be soiled by too much contact with a pariah. The sinking feeling most straight people get when they wander accidentally into a gay bar is a social panic as well as a sexual one. In order to avoid that terror, every interaction with the other must be staged on terms favorable to normals. It's necessary to know that the homosexual is not "us," and also to insist that he or she behave differently from "them"—that is, queers in general.

This may explain why the gay right has such appeal to straights who don't share its political ideology. Liberals like the etiquette, the eagerness to meet their expectations, and the willingness to say what they wish they could about "your kind." But the heart of this alliance is the contempt straight liberals and homocons share for the idea that queers are a distinct people with their own values, practices, and identities. Worse still is the demand that these differences be expressed in public, and that society accept not just a handful of gifted gays but the whole community, stigma and all. Progressives stand for the rise of groups; conservatives for the formation of elites. Liberals may support the former when it involves housing projects and schools, but when it comes to entering their ranks as social equals, they prefer the conservative approach, thank you. They're looking for a few good gays, not an infantry.

Homocons make this selection seem reasonable. After all, as they are always saying, anyone can apply for a place at the table. Those who are accepted deserve it, and so do those who are not. Never mind that there are a limited number of places reserved for each pariah group. The injustice of this arrangement is never raised. Social scarcity is accepted as a fact of life; without it there would be no such thing as prestige, and prestige is the grand prize for the gay right. Theirs is the gatekeeper philosophy of the parvenu. It provides the homosexual gentleman with the tools he will need for success: dedication to the order, disdain for the outcast, and a willful disregard of Oscar Wilde's maxim about the two sources of unhappiness: "not getting what you want—and getting what you want."

Assimilation is a temptation for any pariah group. It's understandable that such people will do what they can to get the weight of stigma off their backs, and it's plausible that, at a time when only some of them can rise, they would leap at the chance to be part of an elite. The gay right has hitched its wagon to this star, just as conservatives in general have made inroads by inviting members of stigmatized groups to think of themselves as special individuals rather than minorities. But this arrangement creates its own anxieties, because it isn't founded on a change in *group* status. The great lesson of Jewish history is that as long as your difference remains an issue, you will share the destiny of your kind. And so the homosexual gentleman is implicated in the drag queen's fate. The f-word and all it represents still hang in the air when he leaves the room.

"A homosexual child raised in a heterosexual family will never be happy," Andrew Sullivan has written, and he holds that politics can't change this fact. Fatalism—the manly way of dealing with fragility—is the dominant mood of the gay right. For them, homophobia is hard-wired into the human condition. Yet my generation has seen the mutability of stigma. As a left-handed boy, I couldn't imagine that such an orientation once inspired the word *sinister*. When I joked about going blind from masturbating, I never considered it a remnant of real beliefs about "onanists," who were once considered a pathological personality type. As a child, I knew all about the onus against single mothers, but my lover's grandchildren don't. Bias may be part of human nature, but its particulars are constructed, and they can be changed. The cure for stigma is politics.

When we fight for liberation, it's not just from violence and discrimination. We also struggle to free ourselves from false assimilation. The wages of that illusion is death in small doses. But the alternative is not alienation. It's individuality, something homocons constantly talk about—except when it comes to homosexuality. Individuality is the difference between being respected as you are and being tolerated because you are what someone else wants you to be. It's the ultimate product of liberation. But it can only appear when the norm expands to meet its variations, so that the "unwanted difference" is only one distinction among many. This is *true* assimilation: The outsider changes, but so does the insider, and a new culture is born from the play of their particularities.

As an American Jew, I live in the (possibly temporary) shelter of just such a synthesis, so I know it's possible. Sexuality may seem like a much thornier problem than religion, but if the myth of deicide can be debunked, so can the cock-and-bull about sodomy. In order for that to occur, though, some queer equivalent of the exchange between Christians and Jews must take place. It would be different from the lopsided dialogue that currently passes for acceptance. That may create a new class of gentlegays even more dedicated than their betters to the straight and narrow, but the true assimilation of homosexuals would produce a whole new model.

The world gay liberation makes would be a place where identity is not a fate, and where gender presentation is a journey rather than a destination. Each of us would mix and match to create a persona. The result wouldn't be the disappearance of masculinity and femininity, or hetero- and homosexuality, but the evolution of these categories into something more nuanced and less hierarchical. This may sound like a fantasia, but a version of it already exists in the queer community. You can see it at events like the Creating Change conference, which I attended last year. Watching this crowd of mostly young people, I was astonished at how comfortable they seemed, how blithely they frisked from butch to femme and beyond, and how different their affects were from the stilted poses that provided my first image of homosexuality. These kids were neither pariahs nor parvenus. They were—at least in the company of their peers—individuals.

Of course, every queer conference is a kind of utopia. Making that world *the* world is a very different matter. We live in a time when such dreams are ridiculed as tiresome, totalitarian, or downright naive. But if no one had dared to imagine a world where homosexuals would throw off the shackles of faggotry, most of us would be wearing those chains today. Odds are I'd still be what I was when the Stonewall riot erupted. Working at *The Village Voice*, whose office was just above the bar, I watched the howling crowd below with no sense that it had anything to do with me. As a married man determined to manage my homosexuality, I was sympathetic to fairies but utterly unable to identify with them. I was a homo-hetero gentleman, and when the revolution came, I turned to my straight colleagues and earnestly said: "I sure hope those people get their rights."

Fifteen years later, as a gay man with a male lover, I sat with an architect of my emergence and asked whether he had any advice for people like me. James Baldwin replied with the measure of someone who took such questions very seriously: "Best advice I ever got was from an old friend of mine, a black friend, who said you have to go the way your blood beats. If you don't live the only life you have, you won't live any life at all." Whether he knew it or not, Baldwin had articulated the enduring goal of gay liberation: to realize the true entitlement of our birthright, which is not virtual normalcy but freedom.

## 3

## VIRTUALLY MACHO

Don't call Camille Paglia a dyke.

Not that she objects to labels. "Italian pagan mythomane" is one she likes, but you can call her "a lesbian with a male brain," as she's described herself. She digs the artful association with the isle of Lesbos, but she's no dyke; not if you mean those women who worship at the "cthonian swamp" of femininity. For Paglia, masculinity is a heroic flight from the mother, while femininity is the tunnel at the end of the light—and lesbianism is the heart of damp darkness: "It's regressive, because they fall back into the mother, and that's why so much lesbian sex is mommy-huggy-kissy. It's ecstatic but infantile; you've never gone forward."

Of course, you don't have to be a lesbian to find infantile ecstasy arousing. It's the essence of hot sex for many women—and men—gay or straight. But for Paglia, sex is all about the hunt, the pursuit, the animus. This primal male aggression is the source of creative intelligence, which gay men, as major mother-fleers, have in spades. "When a man becomes gay," she has quipped, "he gains twenty IQ points." (Obviously she's never met a twinkie.) "When a woman becomes gay, she loses twenty points." (Obviously she's never met a lesbian attorney.) The solution to this problem is to flee from identification with dykes. Paglia's advice to any baby butch headed in that direction is to recover her full nature—by which Paglia means "opening that thing toward men." As she once told an audience of college students: "I'm not saying stop sleeping with women. I'm saying stop being a lesbian."

If this sounds like post-gay identity politics, it's not. Think of the lesbian scene in a straight porn film, where women lap at each other until a rampant man enters the frame, at which point all attention turns to the Real Thing. It's not incidental to Paglia's oeuvre. Though she presents herself as a scholar of desire—channeling Freud, Jung, and other plumbers of the psychic depths—she is basically a writer of erotica who reconstructs the male lesbian fantasy and calls it common sense. You won't find anything in Paglia's work that can't be shown in hetero porn, which is no doubt why she's never urged straight men to locate *their* full nature by "opening that thing" toward other men.

Like any pornographer, Paglia must raise the rod while calming the fears that lurk in the shadows of sex. She does the former by stroking the male ego, and the latter by attacking its perceived enemies. Among them are pussy-whipped liberals, "screeching pseudo-skinhead" gay activists, "feminist Harpies" who want to turn men into eunuchs, and in particular "lesbo holdouts from paleo-feminism." The word *lesbo*, with its male ending, is the giveaway here; it's the term of contempt for a woman who is 24/7 queer. When it comes to female desire, it isn't babes loving babes who pose a threat, but those who spurn the penis when it's offered; who privilege the "swamp" over the sword—or strap on the rapier. This is why, even in the wake of lesbian chic, butch women remain sexual outlaws. Paglia eludes that status by posing as a dyke-hating butch. She wields the sword, but on behalf of its rightful owner. And she creates a mythopoeic cover for men's fears, so they don't have to be faced.

She's been amply rewarded for her loyalty. Paglia may not be a dyke, but she *is* the most famous lesbian writer in America. Certainly she's the only woman living with another woman (and willing to admit it) to pop up on the latest list of America's top hundred intellectuals. Paglia came in at number 66, not far behind Susan Sontag, and one of only fifteen women on the roster. Since it was assembled largely by toting up media mentions, Pagia's presence is no surprise. No academic in the past ten years has garnered more publicity, and her scholarship is not the reason why. Paglia's major accomplishment is her persona, a retro blend of fire, ice, and cruelty in the service of power that makes her seem both rad and trad. She's the pomo incarnation of a traditional lesbian type that had all but disappeared in feminism's wake: the saucy broad whose imitation of masculinity pays tribute to the real thing.

Though Paglia's life story regularly intrudes on her criticism—which of her readers doesn't know about her childhood attempts to play Hamlet?—she's never been candid about the family drama that led her to become a femophobic lesbian. It doesn't take a psychohistorian to deduce that she identifies with the aggressor—and woe to any man who shrinks from playing the conquistador, or any woman who won't strew flowers in his path. This crusade on behalf of masculinity is what ties Paglia to Andrew Sullivan and other homocons. Identifying with male aggression is central to their world-view, and sexual politics is part of the package. The gay right's message, like that of the entire right, is that the power vested in men is justly assigned. This is a sexy message, especially to liberals who have been taught that male power is arbitrary and oppressive, and that identifying with the aggressor is a symptom of neurosis. No way, say Paglia and Sullivan; it's natural.

There have always been gay men and lesbians who identify with what might be called the masculine principle. The performance artist Peggy Shaw weaves a deeply moving monologue around the act of taping up her breasts and changing into her father's clothes. Every drag queen and leather man is a performance artist without a script. But it's one thing to explore the power of gender; quite another to proclaim your fetish as a force of nature. This is the difference between Paglia and the sex radicals whose stance she claims to emulate. In order to fathom her appeal, you have to understand the role of pop intellectuals in liberal society. They preside over guilty pleasures. Not only must they revel in the moment; they must create a rationale that allows the audience to distance itself from the moral meaning of its entertainment. Paglia's job is to pump up the prestige of male aggression by making it seem essential. And benign.

"Every time I cross a bridge, I think, 'Men made that'." Here is a typical Paglia *aperçu* in support of the claim that male power is a force for good. Of course, it's easy to turn that testimonial on its head, as in: Every time I visit a museum of the Holocaust, I think, "Men did that." Such statements lend themselves to parody because they're reductive to begin with. But that's a virtue in a pop intellectual, whose job is to turn pithy phrases that uncomplicate desire. In a liberal society, where identifying with the aggressor is frowned upon, porn is one way to gratify that need; Paglia is another. In both, the sexiness of male dominance becomes nature's way of making women happy. Many liberals are drawn to that fantasy even as they understand its relationship to the brute facts of male power. What they don't want from a critic is complexity that gets in the way of pleasure.

Just as any pornographer knows that realism is the enemy of arousal, Paglia shuns qualifiers, and as a result, many of her assertions are false on the face. Take rape. More than anything else in her repertoire, this subject is what made Paglia a star. She doesn't quite blame women for sexual violence, but she does hold them responsible for behaving in a way that brings it on. To wit: "Every woman must take personal responsibility for her sexuality, which is nature's red flame. She must be prudent and cautious about where she goes and with whom. When she makes a mistake she must accept the consequences and, through self-criticism, resolve never to make that mistake again." Though Paglia hasn't been raped (a distinction she attributes to her "vigilance"), she can proclaim that it's not a life-altering event. "If it is a totally devastating psychological experience for a woman, then she doesn't have a proper attitude toward sex." Paglia's advice to women who are raped: "Pick yourself up, dust yourself off, and go on."

Here the tropes of porn become the facts of life. Rape is lust writ large, part of the real erotic deal and not an instrument of social control. Any attempt to regulate more ambiguous forms of sexual coercion, such as date rape, is a plot to strip men of their endowment. "What feminists are asking," says Paglia, "is for men to be castrated." And just who are these ball-breaking bitches? "They come from a protected, white, middle-class world, and they expect everything to be safe. Notice it's not black or Hispanic women who are making a fuss about this—they come from cultures that are fully sexual and they are fully realistic about sex." In Paglia, as in porn, blacks are fantasy emblems of primal sexuality. They stand for the beast, which is no doubt why black performers are so popular in the porn white people buy.

Are black women less affected by sexual violence? Ask a rape counselor at an inner-city hospital or a battered women's shelter. But then, to Paglia, the whole "battered wife motif" misses the point. "Everyone knows that many of these working-class relationships where women get beat up have hot sex." If they stay with their men, it must be because they are kinky—and what's wrong with that? "How come we can't allow that a lot of these battered wives like the kind of sex they are getting?" Of course, the women who show up at shelters aren't there because they crave abuse, but to mention this obvious fact is to intrude on the romance of the down and dirty that Paglia makes of working-class life. But then, she has no firsthand knowledge of the real thing. Despite the blue collar she flaunts, as the daughter of a professor Paglia grew up to the academy born. For that matter, her knowledge of heterosexual relationships is mediated by the fact that she is, as she likes to say, *hors du combat.*

But pointing out such contradictions is as futile as arguing with her assertions. Most of Paglia's readers know perfectly well that rape is more than just a sexual act confined to women who dress provocatively and go out drinking with men. Nearly a fifth of all women have been raped, and the second-largest risk group is girls between the ages of twelve and fifteen. But in the pornographic imagination, the truths we hold to be self-evident are beside the point.

After all, the central ambition of pornography is not to describe reality but to transcend it. In that respect, porn is a myth to which its devotees subscribe. In the throes of their desire, its clearly absurd scenarios seem like repositories of a deeper truth. But this supernatural aura is merely a reflection of our values. Like all myths, porn embodies two responses to morality: idealization and transgression. This is why porn can be irrational (even horrifying), but feel so right. It's a fiction that corresponds to social facts.

The social fact that inspires Paglia's fiction is the so-called crisis of masculinity. This state of emergency wasn't triggered by a power outage. After thirty years of litigation and legislation, men still hold the lion's share of the world's wealth (and control much of the lioness's share). In the material world, guys rule! But on the symbolic plane of status, a shift has definitely occurred. The prestige of masculinity has taken a beating, and this has led to a loss more keenly felt than understood; a forfeiture not of power but of testosterone.

The latest research on this "male hormone" suggests that its production depends substantially on social prestige. Men of high status—lately christened alpha males—have much more of it than their underlings. When a man wins a fight, his testosterone surges; when he loses, it retreats. A sexually active single man has more of it than one who is monogamous and happily married. Imagine, then, the biochemical implications of the feminist model. Nurturance and cooperation may be the ideal male traits for intimacy, and they have their pleasures for men, to be sure; but the production of testosterone isn't one of them. Paglia's natural man would feel stifled by such a personality if he couldn't find refuge in cutthroat competition, sports, and even war. These are testosterone factories, but they may as well shut down if they don't confer prestige—and, as any sports-channel junkie knows, they don't. Imagine growing up male in a world where the rituals men use to stoke their hormones have lost this capacity, where girls are forging ahead of you in school, where a woman is probably your teacher, perhaps your boss, and maybe your only parent. In such a world, where is the jolt that gives men the intense pleasure they crave, not to mention the incentive for sex and self-assertion they need?

The crisis of masculinity may be symbolic, but its effects are real enough, and not just when it comes to sex. Depression and suicide rates are rising among men as their prestige wanes. These casualties are canaries in the mine of macho, but all heterosexuals are a risk group when it comes to acquired testosterone deficiency syndrome. It certainly accounts for the hot contours of today's youth culture, as adolescents recover the old hormonic rituals, replete with teddies and tattoos. Hip-hop is all about the repolarization of the sexes and the return of the cruel, compelling stud. Aggression toward women, gays, Asians, and other traditionally subaltern groups who have dared to act up is part of the retro sheen. But because ghetto brothers (or wiggers) are doing the bashing, the audience can feel that the vicarious thrill it's getting is actually progressive. This illusion is central to rap music's success, since the average fan is a middle-class white boy. No other segment of society is more ambivalent about the loss of male glory.

After all, feminism is a product of bourgeois society, with its ideals of equity and individuality. It's here that the most sweeping change in sexual decorum has occurred. There's a real expectation that men and women will treat each other as peers, and the more liberal you are, the more likely to embrace this standard. No wonder liberals love misogynistic rap. No wonder Paglia sprang Medusa-like from the liberal middle class. "Before there was feminism, there was Paglia," she has boasted, but in fact feminism made her a star. The blazing trajectory of her career shows how far a gay woman can get by bashing women and gays. Like the black rapper who gives a progressive imprimatur to sadistic pleasure, Paglia is an enabler of liberal lust. Her channeling of the 1960s and its ethic of sexual freedom makes her bitch-slapping and fag-baiting seem like a return to hip roots. She makes it rad to be trad.

Paglia was the original attack queer, the first to say what straight liberals wish they could, and it's been a very well-attended performance from the start. But Paglia's 1990 tome *Sexual Personae* wasn't what sparked the flame. It was her subsequent attack on gay studies, which broadened into an assault on the whole liberal academy. It appeared, a few months after her book was published, in a small journal called *Arion*, and it was promptly picked up by *The Chronicle of Higher Education,* then *The San Francisco Examiner,* and finally *Cosmopolitan.* Why would mass-market publications be interested in this relatively arcane subject? Because Paglia had appeared at the dawn of a new phenomenon: the liberal backlash. Her glory was sealed by a revisionist screed about date rape that ran in the most liberal New York daily, *Newsday.* She soon became a cover story in that user manual of wannabe chic, *New York* magazine. It was called, with knowing irony, "Woman Warrior."

By now, it's clear that the liberal backlash is a movement with real social consequences. But before it became a realpolitik, it began as entertainment, and Paglia was a founding minstrel. Her outré pronouncements raised the wrath of the very people who stood accused of being politically correct, and the more feminists fumed, the more fun liberals had. It was politics as porn, with the same claim to hidden truth and transgressive pleasure. Like porn, Paglia was bad to the boner. Reading her made the heart race. Those images of vital men and vamping women, colliding like monsters from the id of Ayn Rand in a landscape of lust and lingerie, were missing from feminist thought. You might as well compare Phil Donahue to Eminem. Indeed, Paglia was the Eminem of the good life. "Don't quote me," says the proper gent in a cartoon from *The Chronicle of Higher Education.* "Out of context, it might sound a bit Camille Pagliaish."

Not that there's anything wrong with being a pornographer, as Jerry Seinfeld might say. The problem isn't the medium but the message it's allowed to send. Feminist writing can be plenty hot, but you won't find that kind of eros in the average porn film. If the mass market expressed the libido's full capacity, role reversal, identity flux, and real queer fucking would be a regular part of smut. But if the production of testosterone is the point, you need a more rigid repertoire: male aggression unto sadism, male bonding unto gang-banging, male domination unto female subjugation. Still, it's just a jape in the service of a jerk. Porn's presumption of innocence resides in this claim, and so does the hip response to Eminem: His songs are an exploration of forbidden fantasy; you don't live by them, but you dig the *frisson.* And what could be intellectually funkier than the sight of Paglia in Diana Rigg regalia commanding a cable TV audience: "Men, get it up! Women, deal with it!" Here is an indictment and an incitement. Like porn, it both advocates and embodies male arousal. But it's also a design for living.

To wit: *Men are beasts. Sex with them is risky, since women have what they want. A woman's power is her booty, but in striving for social status she has lost the will to shake it. Women are unsatisfied, and so are men. Feminism is frustration. The answer can be found in ancient myths that express the truth about sex. It is eternal and unchanging. We need to return to our nature.*

It's hard to make this case on the rational merits; life provides too much contradictory evidence. But if you can show that myths reflect biology, and that biology is destiny, the scenario doesn't seem so arbitrary; it feels like common sense. Has there ever been a tradition that didn't insist it was more than that? Every hegemony relies on a relationship to the essential, whether it's the divine right of kings or the manifest destiny that commands men to hold the TV remote. All power calls itself an expression of natural law. The sexual backlash would be nothing more than a relief from real life if it weren't legitimized by an ideology of the natural. No wonder a whole genre of pop scholarship has arisen around this mission.

Paglia is the cultural auxiliary of the band led by Lionel Tiger, the anthropologist who makes a case for male dominance by locating it in hunter-gatherer society. Never mind that no one really knows how men and women behaved in primordial times, or that—as the feminist critic Barbara Ehrenreich put in a debate with Tiger—his description of the first society bears a suspicious resemblance to Levittown in 1957. The purpose of this thinking is not to describe human nature but to ascribe social relations to a higher power: biology. This is not just hip entertainment and intellectual speculation. It's a program.

Born of metaphysics, Natural Man soon became an entertainment icon, and when disaster struck on 9/11 he strode forth to fill the need for heroes. In its wake, notes *The New York Times*, "A certain kind of woman is tired of the dawdlers, melancholics, and other variants of genius who would not know what to make of a baseball mitt or a drill press." This upwardly mobile woman—"clever, controlled, prone to overthink"—has discovered a taste for blue-collar butch and its (more suitable) manifestation in men "who make big, impactful decisions." The result, the *Times* reports, is a whole new line of menswear designed to make a *sensitif* look like a stud.

Here, the backlash against feminism becomes a fashion statement—but little attention has been paid to its more tangible effects. A recent survey by the federal government shows that over the past seven years, the salary gap between male and female executives has actually been getting wider. The study focused on industries most likely to hire women, and among those professions, the gap is greatest in communications and entertainment. Female managers in communications now earn 73 cents for every dollar paid to their male colleagues; in entertainment, it's 62 cents—down from 83 cents just a few years ago. Is it a coincidence that these are also the industries where backlash culture is made?

The part gay men (mostly closet cases) play in styling gangsta rappers and other b-boys is a dirty little secret in the record industry. But it's a traditional role for homos. We've been crafting heterosexual icons ever since we were driven from the fold. What would male iconography be without Rock Hudson, James Dean, Randolph Scott, and other stars too litigious to name? What would couture be like without . . . name your favorite designer? Central to this task is the outsider's grasp of gender. Queers understand that it must be constantly invented and coded. Armed with that sense, we make men and women what they are. It may be absurd that a lesbian is the new architect of heterosexuality—the salt on the meat of manhood—but it's a social fact. So is the need to preserve the other against which the sexes can be defined. How to maintain that opposition in an ostensibly liberated time? Ask Camille. Not only does she put the *real* back in real men, but she re-creates the faggot. When gays themselves get to decide who will bear that stigma, it's called assimilation.

Andrew Sullivan adores Camille Paglia. He's been known to call her "God-god," and his ideas about masculinity owe much to her cosmology. So does his attack-queer stance. Both writers police their own with a special severity; both hew to the line that nature makes the sexes what they are; both have a devotional attitude toward macho; and both, despite their venomous barbs, are highly sensitive to criticism. Watching these attack queers pummel the left while crying foul at its counter-punch is like seeing St. Sebastian shoot the arrows while claiming martyrdom.

This paranoia amid privilege is central to conservative style, and it's the perfect accessory for publications liberal enough to include gay writing yet hip enough to embrace the backlash. In Sullivan, *The New York Times* gets both. For the past few years, he's been the major voice in its gay coverage, and in exchange America's leading liberal newspaper has made this spokesman for the gay right a star.

At a paper where finesse is expected even of *fauves*, Sullivan has maintained a tone best described as Paglia Lite. Where she rails at "feminist Harpies," he merely ventures that "a certain type of feminism is partly responsible" for the decline of manhood. (What type of feminism? The kind that "refuses to countenance special treatment for men and boys.") She has no qualms about describing Barney Frank, America's most prominent gay politician, as a "physically repellent specimen of alleged manhood . . . with his puny infant's mouth still squalling for mama's bottle." Sullivan would never use such language in the *Times*, any more than he would call the academy "fagged-out," as Paglia has. In order to find the Camille within him, you have to visit Sullivan's personal website (briefly sponsored by the pharmaceutical industry until his editors objected), or check out his dispatches to the alternative press. As in this lucubration for *The Stranger*, a Seattle weekly: "I'm all for the cult of masculinity. . . . Last time I checked, that was a major reason I thought of myself as homosexual. But when hyper-masculine men tart themselves about like homecoming queens, the entire concept of masculinity is negated. . . . They're big girls in nipple clamps."

Once you accept the premise that men are naturally butch, and that gay men are as endowed with this capacity as any other guys, it's a short step to believing that queers who present themselves as something short of manly are "at war with their nature." So Sullivan has described drag queens and androgynes. Paglia is more generous, perhaps because she has less reason to be defensive about masculinity. For her, androgynes are incarnations of the divine, and drag queens are avatars of female power (without those troubling "maw-like genitalia"). For Sullivan, they're "a very small minority" within an otherwise virile community. He accuses the queer movement of "taking that minority and attempting to define the entire gay world through it." Most homosexuals "embrace their gender," and to this silent majority, Sullivan plays Richard Nixon.

Word is that Sullivan's next book will be about masculinity (though it probably won't be called *Six Crises*). Last June, he gave a preliminary account of his thesis, as it applies to homosexuals, in a pride week lecture under the auspices of the *Times*. It was called "The Emasculation of Gay Politics," and it proceeded from a Paglioid vision of the differences between the sexes: "They're based upon deep biological and psychological realities that are reflected across all cultures and all times. Therefore, to say I don't have to be masculine is to say I don't have to have two legs and hands. We do. That's who we are. We are natural beings." As his audience—mostly gay white men of a certain age and means—listened up, Sullivan proposed a program of gender reclamation that would heal their wounds and culminate in a conservation with their straight brothers. "Every opportunity gay men have to reach out to straight men," he declared, "is an opportunity to change the world."

Of course such a conversation is important, even more for straight men than for gays. But are we to meet as equals, or as high and low men on the totem pole? This is hardly an incidental question; it's the difference between tolerance and true acceptance. But Sullivan never broached it, nor did he acknowledge the importance of talking to women. What Mr. Natural would want to be seen playing with girls? On the playing field, there are words for these cases: sissies, nellies, pansies, fruits. Paglia would be the first to use the ultimate epithet for such boys: *fags*—and in a purely descriptive sense, she'd be right. The word refers to more than just homosexuality; it's also used to humiliate men who don't display their difference from women with sufficient ferocity. As feminists have noted, the markers of this difference are essential to the formation of male hierarchies. Boys monitor each other obsessively for signs of effeminacy, and those without that taint rise highest in the pack. In other words, the order needs fags.

A boy who can't throw a ball or master the requisite male gait becomes a fag whether or not he's homosexual. A girl who *can* do both might find shelter in the designation *tomboy*, but when puberty strikes she must abandon such masculine appurtenances (or at least confine them to the playing field) or risk being considered a dyke. Of course, many of the most masterful tomboys do turn out to be gay, as do many of the least combative boys.

The most common memory among homosexuals is this alienation from the rituals of competence that define gender. It shows up long before sexual desire, often as the first sign that you're "different." The wages of that sin, at least for boys, is physical abuse. This is the playground trauma so many gay men can recall. The queer left holds that the ordeal will end only when straight consciousness has changed. Homocons think this is a futile quest, at best. To them, it's gay consciousness that must change. "The world is one in which we will always be hurt," says Sullivan. "Only you can make yourself feel better." And the way to heal thyself is to reclaim thy masculinity.

It's a compelling idea to many gay men, one that has spawned a proliferation of gay sports leagues. And why not? As Simone de Beauvoir noted, athletics provide a sense of agency, which is why she thought it imperative that girls play sports—as they now do. But when women throw the ball, it's an appropriation; when homos do that, it's a reclamation. The distinction has major political implications. The fact that Mark Bingham, the gay hero of 9/11, was a rugby champ gave his fans an added lift. Here was proof that a gay man can master the butchest of sports. But it's more than a coincidence that Bingham was a Republican. The gentleman jock is crucial to the gay right's image, and a big part of their appeal. In fact, it's central to the *right's* appeal.

Masculinism is what holds the conservative movement together. It makes brothers of fundamentalists and libertarians despite their deep differences. The idea that gay men can now be part of this fraternity is mesmerizing to those who still feel wounded by the playground trauma. Healing the pain by becoming the man that the boy within you couldn't be can seem like liberation. Never mind that, since the wound is social, the only remedy is to create a world where the injury is never inflicted. The pain of that formative rejection will persist in adult life as long as macho remains central to male identity. The solution is to change the structure of masculinity—but that's the last thing homocons want. They're out to bolster the norm by urging gay men not to act like fags—and they're convinced that any homosexual who wants to can behave like a man. Those who do can now be good old boys. Only sissies need to be fags.

Sullivan himself is a survivor of the playground trauma. On the rugby field in his native England, he was pummeled bloody. "My own father, when I couldn't throw a rugby ball, described me as a 'fucking poofter,'" he told his audience at the *Times*. Here is a vivid example of the cruelty that passes for fathering in a macho culture, but Sullivan's response to this painful encounter is revealing: "He meant it, I think, in a relatively constructive way, but it wasn't the happiest moment of my childhood." Just as many traumatized kids see the brutalizer as a loving parent, Sullivan can't locate his anger. He does much better when the target is another pouf, especially one who threatens the male order or fails to meet its standard.

Like Paglia, Sullivan identifies with the aggressor. This is the tie that binds these two writers and locates them on the right. It runs through the paternal line. Paglia has never written about her father, so it's impossible to speculate about his place in her iconic constellation. But with Sullivan, it's clear that, like many gay men victimized by rejecting fathers, his life is a quest for the lost imprimatur of macho.

But not all of us were raised by destructive dads. All sorts of families produce queer kids, and the glory of the gay community is the radical diversity that results. Not every homo yearns to recover his "right to be a man," to use Sullivan's words; lots of us are happy to let that cup pass from our groins. He lives on the queer planet where perfect pecs and a heartless regard are the *sine qua non* of sex, but there are hundreds of gay worlds beyond the buff. While there's always been a gay culture dedicated to glute-on-glute affection, many of us are drawn to a variety of types. Plenty of gay men choose lovers who are soulful sissies, flaming creatures, ripe *papis*, or beamish *boychick*s. As John Lennon famously observed: "Whatever gets you through the night, it's all right." The Sullivan stud muffin and the Paglia lesbian with a male brain are recognizable types in the queer community, but they aren't the norm. There *is* no gay norm. But there *are* more visible personae.

Many gay men who aren't reflexively butch can play the part when they want to or need to. It's a skill that comes with the playground or even earlier, when the first response to an unwanted identification with women is to smother all its signs. And precisely because butch is the official male norm, it's a gay ideal as well. This is the most likely explanation for a phenomenon homocons cite as evidence that most gay people feel "normal." A recent study found that nearly all men who place sex ads in gay papers describe themselves as masculine. (A smaller proportion of women call themselves feminine, but still a majority.) What's more, says the survey, most gays seek the same traits in sex partners. If this were really the case, butch women and femmey guys would be sitting home alone, which they certainly aren't. In fact, butch is the face many gay men show to each other, but not the one they reveal to their lovers. Gay relationships typically involve enormous gender flexibility. Most of us are neither butch nor femme, but variable. So the real issue isn't whether homosexuals are normal, but which roles we feel invited to play.

And these days, the public face of queer culture doesn't belong to a sissy or a diesel dyke. With some notable exceptions, our icons are men and women who would have passed for straight in another time. They are the essence of what society regards as a positive gay image, and they are often the most accomplished homosexuals in life. That their power and prosperity are related to their affect shouldn't come as a surprise. Fidelity to the sexual order is rewarded—and this is especially true in conservative times. Just look at the contest between George W. Bush and Al Gore. More than a few voters were lured to the right by the contention that Gore was not a real alpha male. He spent the campaign desperately trying to shake that image, to no avail. A liberal must overcome the suspicion of being unmanly; a conservative need only confirm the assumption that he has brass balls. Bush's cowboy hat more than overcame his many gaffes, and he even got stud points for being less wonky than the wussy Democrat.

Because gender conformity is so crucial to prestige, anyone who carries it off but still doesn't reap the rewards has good reason to be in pain. This group is Sullivan's natural constituency. Instead of putting the onus on society, he blames the movement for their misery; hence "The Emasculation of Gay Politics." Instead of urging them to challenge the straight world, he invites them to adapt to it—as does Paglia. She tells women they'd be far more fulfilled by focusing on their sexual prowess than by striving for social power. He tells gay men they can be part of the *guyim* if they repudiate their *homokeit.* But just as Jews could never be real Christians no matter how hard they might try, gays will always stand apart in a macho society. After all, the f-word has a second meaning: It stands for the way we have sex. Receptive intercourse is inimical to macho, and as long as that's the case, men who take it up the ass or in the mouth will be treated with contempt, as will women whose desires exclude men entirely. Real female fucking, as opposed to the straight porn variety, demonstrates that masculinity is a role, and it will always be threatening. We will be penalized for our homosexuality no matter how ably we play the gender game.

The few societies where macho and homosex have coexisted—such as Ancient Greece—were notoriously contemptuous of women and effeminacy. There's more than a whiff of those values in Sullivan and Paglia's cosmology. For them, masculinity must be conferred on men by other men, preferably straight ones, in the agony of competition and the ecstasy of bonding. But like so many of their statements, this one is only socially accurate. The natural fact is that every man is masculine, just as every woman is feminine, no matter how they present gender. We cannot fail a test we have no need to take. The very concept is a figment of the male order, and its fundamental purpose is to allocate power. But to someone who couldn't throw the ball to please his father, power in the eyes of straight men is the ultimate consolation, well worth the repression of his full nature.

In one of his more infamous *Times* pieces, Sullivan wrote a testimonial to his testosterone patch. Though it was prescribed by his doctors for the damage caused by HIV, it had a much more comprehensive effect. As his body bulked up, his temperament changed to suit it. "Depression, once a regular feature of my life, is now a distant memory," Sullivan reported. "I feel . . . more persistent, more alive." He's not the first man to discover the joy of a testosterone rush, but not every patient would call his therapy a "manhood supplement," as Sullivan does. In his eulogy to "T," you can glimpse the future of a homocon society. It would be a singularly muscular place, where anyone who didn't fit the mold can be medicated to enhance his masculinity. Forget pec implants; this is an existential makeover. Wear the patch and be jolted into alignment with the man you really are. Now every Pee Wee Herman can become Rock Hudson, every Schubert his own Carl Orff. And what a loss that would be.

Yet if the current backlash goes uncontested, it's not hard to imagine a time when millions of gay men are tempted in this direction. No doubt these *über*homos would lord it over trannies who "mutilate" their bodies, just as upwardly mobile lesbians would frown on "man-hating" dykes. Some women might find it easy to "open that thing toward men," as Paglia suggests, and some men would come all but naturally to their brass balls. But many others would struggle to achieve what drag queens call "realness." Butch would be even more of a closet than it is today. Lesbians would flee from it and gay men would cling to it, terrified that the fag within might show. But the greatest irony is that all of this would be in vain. The signatures of gay macho and lesbian chic would promptly become the new marks of difference. The attempt to create a scapegoat of your own would be futile, since every homo would still be some straight man's faggot.

Meanwhile, the playground trauma would be visited on a new generation of sissies, whose only consolation is to be told by their gay betters that if they hurt, it must be because they lack self-esteem. The prom would continue to be hell for girls who can't follow a boyfriend's lead. And in the highest echelons of gay society—where men are men, and everyone else stays out of sight—there would be a haunting suspicion that we're not the real thing after all. We're virtually macho.

Feminism offers a different model, in which power flows from individuality. The world it would create is one where no one has to butch up or femme down to fly right. Gay people would be free to follow the heart, not to mention the blood, without sacrificing prestige. But this would also be a much healthier place for straights. After all, macho isn't just about fathers passing their glory on to their sons; it's also about fathers injuring their sons and mothers repressing their daughters. In that sense, macho—like the faggotry it requires—is a wound for everyone.

But the wound we know is often easier to bear than the one we fear. This is a truism of psychotherapy, the reason why it's so hard to wean neurotics from their ways. Change is a terrifying project, and what could be more fundamental than altering the way the sexes relate? The rise of women, a major evolutionary moment in human history, is also a source of profound anxiety to women as well as men. The guilt, the foreboding, the sheer panic that come with abandoning a preordained place in the sexual order, are every bit as great as the exhilaration. And since this change in the status of women involves not just sex but every aspect of life, why shouldn't homosexuals feel as anxious about it as anyone else?

No wonder so many of us need the psychic comfort food that the backlash provides. When a crisis strikes, as it did when the World Trade Center went down, we seek the sustenance of these images, and suddenly they become larger than life. The strong-man steps forward from the screen, and everyone flees from perilous agency to the shelter of his arms. In such a climate, identifying with the aggressor seems like a survival skill. No wonder a conservative president can bring Congress to its feet by comparing his own philosophy to that of the 1960s: Then it was: "If it feels right, do it," Bush told a transfixed nation; now it's: "Let's roll!" This is not just a statement about ending permissiveness; it's also about the rewards of privileging male authority—and rest assured, America is now in the hands of authoritarian men.

War organizes more than society; it also provides a structure in which people can organize themselves. These days, you can catch Andrew Sullivan on TV, his identification with the aggressor mobilized by the ultimate T-rush: combat. Patch-powered, he rails against anyone who would tarnish the war effort or violate his standard of patriotism by insisting on making a social critique. The left, he proclaims, is dead—and perhaps he's right if he means the politics of alleviating pain. As for Paglia, aside from a predictable ode to firemen, at this writing she's been silent on the war. Given her opposition to Bill Clinton's Somalian campaign, it's possible that she doesn't like everything she sees. But you know what they say about unintended consequences. And what could be less intended than inspiring a frightened people to escape from freedom—and into pornography.

4

FIGHTING THE GAY RIGHT

Close readers of Norah Vincent, the lesbian avenger of the right, were struck by her column in the year-end issue of *The Advocate*, America's largest gay weekly. Vincent is a protégée of Andrew Sullivan, but now she took a potshot at her conservative mentor, lumping him with queer progressives and blaming them one and all for the "falsely polarized views" that have riven gay politics. In fact, Vincent proclaimed, "the gay culture wars are over."

Even for an adept careerist, this was cheeky. After all, Vincent had made her mark as a writer by skewering the left, along with the less assimilable members of her tribe. Transsexuals, lesbians without a sense of humor, and gay men who live for sex all were targets of Vincent's coruscating barbs. These sallies had endeared her to raffish liberal publications like *The Village Voice* and *Salon*. But in *The Advocate*, she was all sweetness and lite. She might have regaled her straight readers with potshots at the city of San Francisco for adding sex-change surgery to its roster of health benefits, but in the gay press she was willing to let a thousand trannies bloom. "Normal," she now proclaimed, "is just a cycle on a dishwasher." And as for those polarizing political labels, they were never accurate to begin with. How could Camille Paglia, a registered Democrat, be a member of the gay right? Fire-breathing right-wingers like Sullivan had merely "said what needed saying at a time when no one else was saying it." But now it's time to forge a new middle course: "not conservative, not liberal. Just solid center." Vincent offered herself as the Madeleine of this new way.

This repositioning is hardly a new tactic. In the Punch and Judy Show that passes for American political debate, paleocons often call themselves "classic liberals," while casting liberals as the new Commies. The effect of that strategy is to shift the entire political spectrum to the right. But the ultimate conservative weapon is insisting there's no longer any reason to think in terms of left and right. These labels belong on the junk heap of European history, from whence they came. Here in the land of the free, there's only "common sense"—that is to say, the reigning orthodoxies.

But pulling off this legerdemain in the queer community is harder than it might seem. Here, the terms *left* and *right* have a particular meaning. It's not just political ideology that defines your place on the spectrum; it's how you stand on issues such as sexual freedom, mainstreaming, and gender equity. By this measure, it's quite accurate to describe writers like Paglia, Sullivan, and Vincent as the gay auxiliary of the backlash against feminism and identity politics. They may aptly be called homocons.

Yet the hard truth is that many middle-class gays and lesbians agree with Vincent when she casts queer politics as one big hissy fit. They find the gay culture wars arcane at best and irrelevant at any rate. They're not likely to be busted for balling in the park, they aren't tempted to dress for transsex, they don't feel violated by *Will & Grace* or exercised by the absence of black faces from their movement's leadership. In short, these homos *moyens sensuels* aren't heavily invested in issues that animate the queer left. But neither are they creatures of the gay right.

What they are is acutely political. Middle-class lesbians and gay men give heavily to campaigns and vote in large numbers— usually for Democrats. Unlike homocons, they see the value of laws against discrimination, and not only for themselves. They tend to support affirmative action for women and minorities, as well as environmental causes and gun control, and they are far more likely than the general population to identify themselves as liberal. Ralph Nader did quite well with gay voters in the last presidential election. Yet this constituency is more receptive than its politics might suggest to the allure of homocons.

One reason for their fascination is that gay conservatives are in tune with the time. They come off as unrepentant individuals, tapping into the popular myth that each of us is responsible for our destiny. They exploit the enduring shame around gender nonconformity by proclaiming a place at the table for any queer who cleans up his act. (As for *her* act, they presume it's clean to begin with.) And they offer the ultimate solace for prodigal gay progeny: reconciliation with the father in the form of straight male society. Yet as troubled by their alienation as gays who yearn to return to the patriarchal fold may be, they are hardly unique in that respect. The passion to conform is far more intense these days than the urge to rebel. As queer theorist Michael Warner has observed, normalcy is to Americans what glory was to Ancient Greeks. To the extent that normalcy is associated with upward mobility, it's almost irresistible to middle-class gays. Before they were homosexual, they were raised to strive, and by embracing this ambition, the gay right seems as American as the queer left seems alien for its critique of that desire.

No wonder homocons are so successful when they present themselves as just plain folks while casting radicals as a class-baiting, male-berating, Streisand-hating elite. This is not so different from the image that the right has foisted on the left in general. It has marginalized all sorts of progressive thinking, while making reactionary ideas seem populist—but in this case it's not entirely inaccurate. The queer left is profoundly aware of race, class, gender, and the way these attributes create social hierarchies. Homocons prefer to pretend that such differences don't really matter. For them, gay rights have nothing to do with social justice and everything to do with getting the government off your back. So they focus on issues of "civil equality" such as marriage and service in the military. As far as this agenda goes, it's enormously popular with gay and lesbian strivers regardless of whether they intend to enlist or wed. Not only are these rights reserved for heterosexuals, but they are important signifiers of social status—which is precisely why they divide the queer left.

Every time I report on same-sex marriage, I'm struck by how many lesbian-feminist attorneys are dedicated to this fight. But it's also true that the most articulate critique of marriage has come from queer and feminist radicals who regard matrimony as an instrument of oppression. The issue has come to a head in the gay community now—not just because it threatens to siphon money and energy away from other items on the political agenda, such as anti-bias laws, but because same-sex marriage epitomizes the larger question of normalcy. You can't talk about it without addressing its impact on the distinct structure of queer society. In his book *The Trouble With Normal*, Warner eloquently describes this domain, "with all its variations from the norm, with its ethical understanding of those variations, with its ethical refusal of shame or implicitly shaming standards of dignity, with its refusal of the tactful silences that preserve hetero privilege, and with the full range of play and waste and public activity that goes into making a world." This anarchical milieu seems in some sense dependent on the fact that queers can't form classes based on marriage.

But there's a radical critique of this critique, from activists who insist that people can take an oppressive institution and make something new of it. Surely the leftist idea of cultural resistance applies to marriage, these activists maintain. Would gay people do it the way it's supposed to be done, or would they create a new way that honors all sorts of arrangements? And why wouldn't the model that gays invent influence their straight peers? This is just what the homophobes fear: that same-sex marriage would open the door to legal recognition for all sorts of unions. Sullivan's counterclaim, that gay matrimony would *bolster* the norm, is precisely what anti-marriage radicals fear. But there's a third possibility: that the norm would expand to include the variations that actually correspond to many people's lives.

As this argument rages, it doesn't preclude a consensus among radicals that as long as the option of marriage exists, it ought to be available to lesbians and gays. And so, many queer leftists find themselves in the unenviable position of arguing against a practice while supporting the right to do it. This ambivalence has left a clear playing field for homocons. Not only has it enhanced their credibility among gay strivers, but it's brought them face to face with the national gay movement for the first time. Now they can present themselves as enablers of freedom, while casting radicals as puritans who want to tell people how to live rather than helping them live the way they want to.

The gay right's courtship of the strivers couldn't be more consequential. Much has been made of the power wealthy funders and gay-friendly corporations wield, but as a 1998 study revealed, 83 percent of the money donated to gay groups comes from people who earn $75,000 or less. It's likely that most of those donors are middle-class. They are the backbone of our movement, and their instincts are essentially liberal even in this reactionary time. But as gay people respond to new opportunities presented by their success, the longstanding alliance between the center and the left is fraying. Same-sex marriage is a wedge issue. It signals a major rift between radicals and strivers, one the homocons are out to promote. They want to wean the gay mainstream from its affiliation with the left, and unless their efforts are met by a strong progressive response, they may succeed. That would mean more than just the forfeiture of yet another liberal constituency. It would mean the end of a way of thinking about sex, self, and society that has been a major force in progressive sensibility.

The Millennium March on Washington was a telling reminder of just how far the gay mainstream has drifted from its radical moorings. Despite the futuristic vibe of the rally's title, family values were the order of the day, and corporate banners were the major talismans of liberation. During the planning meetings, there were walkouts by people of color and other progressives, and after the march a scandal erupted over the funds that had been raised. These were signs that the gay movement—or at least, this wing of it—had sadly come of age. But in fact, many activists who helped put the march together were radicals in their home states. I interviewed one such organizer, a Chicana from Texas, who had spent years lobbying for a hate-crimes bill that included gay people, only to see it tabled at the last minute after lobbying by the governor, George W. Bush. She was no homocon; nor did she approve of everything the march's sponsor, Human Rights Campaign, stood for. After HRC backed Republican Al D'Amato over Democrat Charles Schumer in the 1998 New York senatorial campaign (and Schumer won), more than eyebrows were raised in the gay and lesbian community. HRC was forced to run a gauntlet of outrage.

Still, HRC remains the wealthiest gay political organization, followed by the more modestly endowed—and more progress-ive—National Gay and Lesbian Task Force. Perhaps the major difference between these groups is their attitude toward identity politics. NGLTF is more open to queers who look and act the part, while HRC hews to the dress-for-success code of the striver. But when it comes to movement politics, both groups have the same basic agenda: They support same-sex marriage *and* laws against discrimination, which puts them squarely in the gay mainstream—and the liberal wing of the Democratic Party. A foundation formed by the Log Cabin gay Republicans recently placed ads in major papers accusing the national movement of promoting "virtual victimhood" by pushing for anti-bias statutes. That didn't earn them many friends; nor did Sullivan's complaint that these groups are run by girls, ferchrissake! Every now and then, the fangs show beneath the finesse, reminding main-streamers of just who their friends are, and what the right intends.

But the gay movement is kept on track by more than just a program. It's tied to the left because it sprang from the left—or, more precisely, from the marriage (if you will) between bohemi-anism and socialism more than a century ago. This heady union begat a sensibility long before it produced an agenda, and gay lib-eration was part of it almost from the start. The ability to make connections between sexual repression and social oppression is a signature of the democratic left, and it owes a great deal to the dreams and schemes of utopians, many of whom were gay.

Literature was the first arena where the implications of homosexuality were addressed, and most of the writers who ventured to do so were leftists. Their political beliefs were inflected by their sexuality, and vice versa. The result was a distinct aesthetic, socially acute and earnestly romantic, albeit laced with irony. Camp may be the most famous marker of gay style, but this progressive aesthetic is far more central and enduring. The power of a play like Tony Kushner's *Angels in America* is not just its passionate response to AIDS, but the way it resonates with the gay visionary tradition. That sensibility, with its faith in desire, in the bonding sex creates, in the sanctity of those bonds and their liberating potential, is queer humanism.

The critic Harold Bloom has made it fashionable to speak of "the anxiety of influence" artists feel toward past masters, but there's been precious little thinking about the communion of gay artists and the way they pass along values. There's a link between Walt Whitman and Allen Ginsberg, Oscar Wilde and Fran Lebowitz, Marcel Proust and Jeanette Winterson, Gertrude Stein and John Kelly, Carson McCullers and k.d. lang, Tennessee Williams and Rufus Wainwright (or, if you prefer, Dusty Springfield). It would be wrong to infer that these artists share a politics, or anything like a common style. But they do share a certain temperament, a sensitivity to the complexities of desire, a perspective on society. And, broadly speaking, nearly all these artists are part of the left.

It's one thing to speculate about whether Schubert's music reflects his homosexuality; quite another to explore its relationship to the poetics of Tennessee Williams—but there is one. It's easier to see *Queer As Folk* as pure product than an image out of *Democratic Vistas*—but Whitman's desideratum for democracy and Showtime's gay sitdram are joined at the johnson. When Whitman wrote about the "thruster who holds me tight and who I hold tight," he was referring not just to a lover but to "adhesiveness," his word for a brotherhood founded in desire. I think Whitman would have appreciated *Queer As Folk*. At its core is the adhesiveness of gay friends, of mothers and gay sons, of lesbians and gay men. The same society appears in Armistead Maupin's *Tales of the City*, and it's not just a fictional creation. It exists wherever people live out Whitman's observation about the greatest lesson to be drawn from nature: "variety and freedom." This lesson is the essence of queer humanism, and it remains the ethos of the queer community.

We were a work of art before we were a people, and we still invest culture with a special meaning. It's the arena where we mourn our losses, where we explore the social aspects of our sexuality, where we invent personae and make style. No wonder the debate over gay visibility in the mainstream is so intense. Culture is to queers what religion is to Jews: the matrix of our nation. This living tradition still shapes our politics, even though the conditions that produced it have changed. This is why many gays, like many Jews, retain a liberal inclination regardless of their economic status. It's a source of endless frustration to the gay right, which argues that the real home for homos is libertarian conservatism. Why would gay strivers who aspire above all to be normal still feel bound to the left? The answer is tradition. Culture has its reasons that self-interest does not know, and our culture grounds us in progressive values. In some sense, you can't be a queer humanist and a homocon. The gay right exists, just as Jews for Jesus do, but it stands apart from the sensibility that marks us as a people.

Central to this sensibility is a critique of male power that goes back a long way before queer theory. You can find the same insights that animate Eve Kosofsky Sedgwick's landmark study, *The Epistemology of the Closet*, in *Cat on a Hot Tin Roof.* Tennessee Williams understood the relationship between the patriarchy and the repression of female and homosexual desire; he knew why the good old boys in *Orpheus Descending* castrate the snakeskinned lover who unleashes the passions of an old man's oppressed wife. If gay people view sexual politics in a certain way, it's largely because artists like Williams created gay consciousness. And they, in turn, drew their perceptions from a particular set of experiences that came with being homosexual.

Everything about the gay milieu before Stonewall reflected a skewed relationship to status, so that, as segmented as the Life might be, it also produced a sense of shared destiny. If you lived outside the major cities, it was even easier to deduce that the fates of sissies and studs, drag queens and diesel dykes, lesbians and gay men were linked, because you might run into all these people in the same bar. The Stonewall Inn was an urban equivalent of those dives, a refuge for queers who couldn't qualify for admission to the more exclusive gay bars dotting Manhattan. The ethic of inclusion that drives the gay right crazy arose from this democratic ambiance. But there has always been another impulse in gay life, a desire to create a world restricted to your own kind.

In the 1970s, when sex was the emblem of liberation, this urge to create a mirror-image produced a new gay type known as the clone. He was out, proud, and very middle-class, and the culture he crafted was dedicated to the pursuit of exclusivity. In addition to the traditional array of leather bars, wrinkle bars (for the chronologically challenged), hustler bars and such, there were now blond bars, clubs where patrons had to squeeze past barriers designed to weed out the overweight, discos with steel mesh staircases to keep out drag queens in high heels, and plenty of chic gay venues with quotas for women. Though the disco culture was ostensibly defined by what novelist Andrew Holleran called "the democracy of the dance," this egalitarian aspect of clone life couldn't compete with the need to be part of an elite. The result was a *polis* of the pumped. Yet, as narcissistic as this society seemed, it wasn't just driven by vanity. Clones were attempting to create status in the only way out gay men could in those days: through sex and style.

There was a (far more flannel) lesbian equivalent of this impulse toward exclusivity: a move to separate from men that also drew a distinction between "realesbians" and "politicalesbians," as experimenting feminists were called by purists. This tendency still survives, as transsexuals excluded from the

Michigan Womyn's Music Festival can attest, but it has never dominated lesbian politics. One reason is the profound connection with queer humanism; another is the lesbian response to the AIDS crisis, when, as critic C. Carr notes, "we were losing our long-lost brothers." AIDS brought the posh project to a halt by putting all queers in basically the same boat. But now that the epidemic has relented somewhat, the old urge to distinguish ourselves from ourselves has returned. This time, the hot-button issue isn't separatism or the tyranny of buff, but real world status and how to raise it. As the stakes grow more tangible, the quest for exclusivity is becoming politicized.

Homocons are an ideological update of the gay clone. Though the uniform has changed, the impulse to create an elite remains the same. Everything about the attack-queer persona—its proclamation of "gender patriotism," its ceremonial respect for macho, its contempt for "group-think"—is designed to distinguish homocons from the queer herd. And this style is the secret of the right's appeal to strivers (especially of the male persuasion). It's not the politics that attracts them, but the attitude. The attack-queer stance is compelling because it's butch, and butch is status, especially in a time of backlash.

The gay clone was nothing if not butch. He borrowed his attire from the jeans-and-T-shirt look of regular guys. Of course, straight men soon fled from the haberdashery that homos had appropriated. They even adopted boxer shorts to distinguish themselves from fags who favored briefs. But times have changed: Gay style is no longer anathema to ambitious straight boys, while the business suit has become the *sine qua non* of gay male assimilation. This crossover is a sign that the onus is shifting, at least in sophisticated circles, from homosexuality to gender discordancy. The gay right is eager to meet this new standard. When Sullivan speaks of virtual normalcy, a big part of what he means is summed up in his exhortation to "embrace your gender." For lesbians, that means learning to be glamorous; for gay men, it means reclaiming your "natural" masculinity. If some of us can't or won't do that, so be it. The gay right is more than willing to segment the queer community. After all, what would status be without scarcity—and status is what homocons are all about.

Their vision is the clone's dream come true, except that now it doesn't depend on shaking your booty. It's about a possibility homosexuals have never been presented with, except in exchange for being closeted: prestige. This is an offer many gay and lesbian strivers can't refuse.

Material as the benefits of matrimony and military service may be, these are also powerful status symbols. That's why the religious right is dedicated to reserving them for heterosexuals. What's at stake is not the dignity of marriage or the cohesion of the fighting unit, but the preservation of prestige. That's something fundamentalists have had to struggle for; no wonder the advance of the gay pariah caste is a *casus belli* for them. Yet, in a nation where status politics *is* politics, no one can afford to ignore a gay constituency that gives every evidence of organized activity.

Republicans are not unaware of the profit in being homo hip, especially in liberal enclaves.

Wearing drag can cover a host of sins, at least in New York City, as Rudy Giuliani demonstrated with his begowned performances at press roasts. His decision to room with two of his friends, a male couple, during his divorce proceedings further endeared Giuliani to this overwhelmingly Democratic constituency. The lesson hasn't been lost on the more conservative state leadership of his party, which is preparing to abandon its longstanding opposition to a gay rights law. Meanwhile in Massachusetts, the Republican governor, Jane Swift, hoped to compensate for her opposition to same-sex marriage by running with a gay lieutenant on her slate (she ultimately withdrew from the party primary in deference to a straight man).

Of course, there will be limits to this flirtation as long as the Republican Party is chaperoned by the Christian right. But the dalliance is real enough, and it has galvanized the homocon political network. A newly formed Republican Unity Coalition, which boasts former senator Allan Simpson as its honorary chair, aims to court "people with established, sometimes powerful ties" to the Party. The group hopes to raise $1 million by next year for a Political Action Committee that will seed the coffers of Republican candidates "who want to see their party get over the issue of sexual orientation, just like it got over the issue of color" (a highly debatable claim). Among its likely recipients is Richard Riordan, the leading Republican candidate for Governor of California.

Meanwhile, as Doug Ireland has reported in *The Nation*, the Liberty Education Foundation, a newly formed arm of the Log Cabin Republicans, is "soliciting large contributions from national gay groups and well-heeled AIDS organizations on the grounds that 'we have access' to the Bush administration." (They've reportedly asked HRC for $200,000.) Ireland also noted a connection between the Independent Gay Forum (IGF), which runs a website for homocons, and BQ Friends, "a secret, exclusive e-mail listserv network" that takes its name from an anthology called *Beyond Queer: Challenging Gay Left Orthodoxy.* According to Ireland, this entity is about to become "a full-service political operation" under the auspices of a former aide to Secretary of Health and Human Services Tommy Thompson. (IGF, by the way, is run by a former consultant to Defense Secretary Donald Rumsfeld.)

While the prospect of a *rapprochement* between the gay community and the Republican Party may seem politically propitious, it doesn't come without a price. Consider this excerpt from the mission statement of the Republican Unity Coalition: "Neither victim nor villain, we seek no special privilege, but we deplore being penalized. Many of us simply want to be left alone." This coded manifesto suggests how homocons would change gay politics. No more lobbying for laws against discrimination and hate crimes (i.e. special rights); and as for sexual freedom, consider RUC's credo: "We are committed to a respect for the faith of the Founders [and] we recognize the value and importance of moral and ethical standards." Next time gays are busted for cruising in the park (or accepting a proposition from a plainclothes cop), who will represent them? Who will act up when the government allows church groups to fire gay social service workers? Certainly not a movement that increasingly finds its interests tied to a right-wing elite.

When neoconservatives undertook the task of winning over a largely liberal electorate in the late 1970s, the first thing they did was to direct funding from wealthy right-wingers to institutes, publishing houses, and magazines that expressed their point of view. Then they found writers who were scathing in their contempt for liberalism and adept at tapping the resentments of the middle class. As the backlash gathered steam, they beefed up their ideology in tabloids like the *New York Post*, set up their own cable news network (FOX), and bought liberal publications that had fallen on hard times. (The latest example of this tactic is the purchase of *The New Republic* by associates of the neocon Manhattan Institute.) The gay right is taking a page from this manual on building a new majority. They are funding writers, placing them in gay and mainstream papers, making alliances with big-money donors, and training spokespeople to reach out to wavering liberals.

The war against terrorism has only intensified this process, as quasi-government foundations seek to disarm potential pockets of dissent on college campuses and, yes, in the queer community. One such group, The Foundation for the Defense of Democracy, headed by a former communications manager of the Republican National Committee, recently appointed Norah Vincent as a senior fellow.

The last time she appeared on *Politically Incorrect*, she looked and sounded like someone who had been coached by professionals. Gone was the punky dyke who once graced the offices of *The Village Voice*. Now she wore a soft, semi-clinging sweater, twinkled at Bill Maher, the host, and never mentioned feminists or trannies. Instead, she spoke as a common-sense patriot with libertarian leanings. This is an attack queer whose time has come.

The question is: Has the queer left's time passed? That depends in part on how radicals address the rise of homocons. Too many gay progs regard them as beneath contempt. Too many activists think the movement should focus its attention on the "real enemy." Too many liberal foundations ignore the importance of funding gay and lesbian publications. Too many hetero lefties regard gay liberation as a middle-class phenomenon destined to move rightward with the rest of the bourgeoisie. This combination of fatalism and myopia is the ideal matrix for a well-armed backlash. It has enabled the gay right to encircle the queer movement as it sleeps. And unless progressives awaken to this threat, the thing that is beneath contempt will soon be beyond control.

Imagine a time when major funding for national gay groups comes from the right. Bizarre as that may seem, it's quite possible. If the Log Cabinite foundation can boast of an "official and exclusive airline" (United), why couldn't Big Pharm and other "gay-friendly" industries serve as agents of a Republican Party that won't own up to its interest in homosexuals, but can't afford to resist them? After all, the Democrats raised $18 million from the gay community last year. That ain't rubbers.

But mining the movement is only part of the gay right's agenda. Homocons are also out to shatter its cohesion. When Sullivan urges gay men to create a movement of their own, he's not just talking about banging drums in the forest. As he surely knows, if gay men formed a *frauenrein* movement, it would have a dramatic effect on everyone else. Since white gay males are wealthier than lesbians, their secession would leave women—not to mention most blacks and marginalized queers—to make the most of a much smaller pie. Even in fat times, the gay movement is given to schisms; it comes with the territory of oppression. But as money grows scarce for progressive causes, the clashing of out-groups inevitably would intensify. Pat Buchanan once boasted that AIDS would destroy the gay movement, but there's a more plausible possibility: fragmentation as an unintended consequence of success.

The breakup of the gay community is not beyond conceiving. After all, there are many models for homosexuality (and many homosexuals who defy every model). Countless queer worlds, not all of them salutary, have existed, and new worlds, brave or craven, are possible. We could be headed for a time when the gay equivalent of the "high yellow"—a butch man or femme woman with just a touch of the homo tarbrush—rises to some semblance of respectability. Like all people whose status is precarious, the last thing these parvenus would want to be reminded of is their affiliation with those who can't pass. Deviant *déclassés* are anathema to the virtually normal.

I caught a glimpse of this future recently when the gay gentry in my neighborhood, Greenwich Village, demanded that the nightly congregation of banjee boys and hustling trannies (most of them black) be driven from the local waterfront. Never mind that this stretch of the Village has been home to all sorts of sexual carousing for more than a century. The historian Allan Bérubé speculates that Herman Melville cruised these docks when he worked at the nearby customs house. But that landmark has become a pricey residential property, and now that the buff white boys who once made this area a gay agora have moved to other precincts, the issue of probity arises. "This has nothing to do with gayness," one lesbian crusader told a sympathetic reporter from the *The New York Times*. That's only partly a lie. It has *everything* to do with gayness as it once was, and little to do with what it's becoming.

Trans activists have been saying all along that the way we have sex isn't the real reason we're oppressed; it's the way we present gender. That contention seems more credible as homosexuals reach for respectability, and it has sparked a new debate in the queer community. Some radicals think the acronym that describes us should be changed to a more appropriate term. They would call it the gender rights movement, and in the current situation their proposal could come to pass. We may see a "gay" movement run by an assimilated elite and a "gender" movement representing the unassimilable. Certainly it's a tempting alternative to the current endlessly shaky arrangement, but neither of these entities would be as powerful as the imperfect amalgam they left behind. As a fragmented community, we'd be much less able to fight the power—and that would suit the right just fine.

If the queer community is to survive in its current form, it must face the coming identity crisis. The left is well positioned to lead this reckoning because of its grounding in the tradition that has always held gay people together. Queer humanism is rich enough and imbedded enough in our consciousness to withstand the acidic effects of assimilation. But precisely because it's an ethic of low status, a way of transforming disgrace into grace, it has never contemplated a situation in which some of us can rise without dissembling while many more cannot. What would E.M. Forster make of a time when Maurice's problem isn't that he's attracted to a male servant, but that he's a nance? What would Tennessee Williams make of the day when Orpheus descends to his own Showtime special?

I don't mean these questions to be as fanciful as they may seem. People are shaped by tradition, but not bound by it. The ethos that ties the gay community to the left can be lost, and so can the clarity about our situation that it provides. If the insights of queer humanism are to guide a generation that has never had to depend on the kindness of strangers, the left must renew its own tradition. A good motto for that task would be Forster's deeply queer exhortation: "Only connect."

The activists I most admire—and the most successful ones, I think—have a certain attitude in common: a respect for aspiration. They don't try to create the new man and woman, they help real people rise. After all, ambition is one of the great motivating forces in human history, and all civil rights movements unleash it in their members. These activists are willing to take the risk that banality will be the result of their success. And they grasp the reason why oppressed people often express their ambition in grotesque ways. The parvenu is both the beneficiary and the victim of an ambivalent embrace, as recent queer history attests. Perhaps the gay clone would have acted on his egalitarian impulses if he hadn't faced such a battle for acceptance. Perhaps the attack queer would be less cruel if the world were truly open to us all.

The gay movement has always had its strivers. The alliance of middle-class warriors with drag queens and downcast queers is what gave gay liberation its power. As a result, our agenda has always been twofold: to create an alternative to straight society— what Warner calls "the world-building project of queer life"—and to "move on up," in the Jeffersons' immortal words. The symbols of upward mobility were different in the early days: to run for office, to reveal the homosexuality of great men and women, to get the press to use the word *gay* (no easy task at the *Times*, where the first response from one of its owners was: "Not in my newspaper!"). But there's a link between these formative struggles and the current fight for marriage rights. Though this issue is often framed as a bid for normalcy, it would be more accurate to call it a quest for prestige. The essence of oppression is being restricted in the pursuit of status, and marriage is the most complex status symbol of all. Being denied access to it is a powerful sign that we are still oppressed.

That's why same-sex marriage seems so important for many gay activists at this point in our history. It stands for civic striving, which is not the same as social climbing. This is a crucial distinction, one that requires progressives to support the right to do what they may not think is right. If a single principle sums up our movement, it's that we ought to have the same options as straights. Critics of marriage can work for the day when people reject this institution, but they must also struggle for a time when people make that choice because they are free to, not because they must.

There's a dark side to the marriage crusade. It could lead to an abandonment of queers whose desires take them in a different direction, especially if gay strivers accept the message that sexual transgressors threaten their prestige. Among states with sodomy laws, there's a growing support for replacing them with statutes that would decriminalize homosex in private while upping the ante for public sex—even making it a felony. This "solution" would create a new basis for inequality (unless you think the public sex provision would be enforced in heterosexual lovers' lanes), but don't expect homocon fighters for "civic equity" to object. A Virginia Log Cabinite recently wrote a piece for *The Washington Post* promoting this new bill as "common sense." In fact, it's a new way to drive a wedge into our community by separating its members along moralist lines—and we are vulnerable to this form of attack.

Our relationship to each other has always been a tricky one, given the fact that we don't share a class background or even a set of sexual tastes. As long as we were all outcasts, the issues that swirl around morality could be dismissed as divisive, but now that we're dealing with real-world status they are crucial. The community's cohesion hinges on our respect for one another's sexual choices and the patterns of intimacy that result. If we build a hierarchy around desire, it will be hard to preserve a sense of common destiny, and without it our power to protect and propel each other will be severely compromised. There's a queer version of the temptation enunciated most eloquently by Father Bonhoeffer: First they came for the sluts, and I said nothing. . . .

The movements best able to withstand the erosive effects of success are those with a bond between radicals and strivers. This mutual regard is the main reason why the black middle class, despite its uplift faction on the right, remains progressive. In the queer community, there's a very different dynamic at work: The left sends a mixed message about upward mobility, and the upwardly mobile respond to the left in kind. The gay right has taken full advantage of this disjunction, yet it's not inevitable, since liberationist ideas are fully consistent with achieving power. Progressives insist that the whole queer community (indeed, all people) must rise; that's their fundamental difference from the right—and it's marked our movement from the start. The question is whether strivers will continue to identify with this larger agenda. It's hard for hungry people to forgo a place at the table until others are invited to dine, but it's possible. A lot depends on how the tradition that consoled us in oppression relates to our emergence.

"By confusing a man with what he possesses," Oscar Wilde wrote, bourgeois society has "harmed individualism and obscured it. . . . so that man thought the important thing was to have, and did not know that the important thing is to be." These sentiments have lost their socialist ring, but they still resonate with the aspirations of Wilde's multitudinous descendants. When we are honored for what we are—or rather, for what we choose to be—that is liberation. Most gay strivers understand this. They're willing to hold out for the real thing even as they take what they can get.

And most gay strivers cherish the occasions when they intersect with a tradition that makes them more than the sum of their accomplishments. You can see it in the energy they devote to gay history, in the patronage they bestow on queer artists, in the intensity with which they pursue gay politics, in the fuss they make over gay holidays. But liberal society has placed them at a crossroads. They are invited to rise and instructed to abandon what makes them distinct. Whether they will see the trick clause in this contract depends in no small part on the credibility of those who can clarify the difference between true and false acceptance. That's a role radicals must play, before it's too late.

What slick beast strides toward Stonewall to be born? Fight the right or wait and see.